Geology Explained

Virginia's Fort Valley
and Massanutten
Mountains

William G. Melson

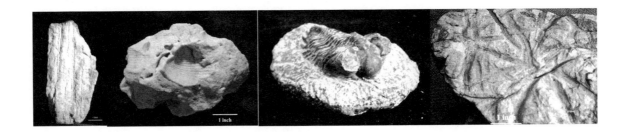

Fort Valley Geology Study Center

Published by InterPress, U.S.A
14056 Fort Valley Road
Fort Valley, Virginia 22652, USA
http://interpressusa.com

2004 Edition

Cover: Buzzard Rock, an outcrop of the Silurian Massanutten Sandstone, folded to nearly vertical. Ridge crest along the Buzzard Rock Trail, near the north end of Massanutten Mountain, Lee District of the George Washington National Forest.

Table of Contents

Foreword

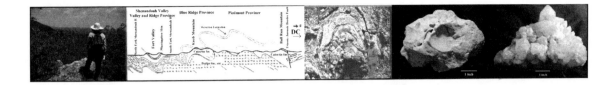

What other guides do for plants and animals, the Geology of the Massanutten Mountains does for the rocks, soils, and terrains that form the surface from which springs the Massanuttens' vast wealth of living things. With this book, Dr. Melson has provided a doorway into a whole new dimension of this singular region, making it possible for us to journey deep into the past, and back again with a new understanding of the land in our own time.

Interpreting the Massanuttens' geological code, the book reveals the story of life forms now lost, and eras when the region was almost inconceivably different. Suddenly, our trips on the roads and trails of the Massanuttens plunge us into the Earth's own restless, ever-changing journey. Through this book, we learn to see telltale remnants of seas that encroached and receded, of mountains that rose and eroded away, of a great delta that once covered what is now a multi-state region, and of the processes of chemistry and climate that carved their own image into the land.

Whether one explores the Massanuttens on walks or on weekend drives, this book will become a companion to translate what is seen along the way; and for the recreational reader it will provide a richly illustrated armchair experience of the region as well as of the science of geology.

–Karen Gray, Ph.D.

Preface

A long, linear ridge is obvious from every west facing overlook along the Skyline Drive in the Northern and Central Sections of Shenandoah National Park. The ridge marks the western margin of the Shenandoah Valley along the South Fork of the Shenandoah River. There are a few minor peaks and gaps along the ridge but, overall, it is remarkably flat. This is Massanutten Mountain—the east lip of the Fort Valley. The ridges and valleys to the west are a remarkably beautiful and fascinating area that is mainly in the Lee District of the George Washington National Forest. The Massanutten Trail, one of the longest and best trails of the area, runs along the crest of Massanutten Mountain. The Mountain and nearby ridges and valleys are the subject of this book. Interwoven into their story are some basic principles of geology that deepen our appreciation of these ancient rocks and mountains. This book may be useful for students who are taking an introductory course in the earth sciences, especially as an aid for fieldtrips to the area or to the Appalachians in general. There are many footnotes concerning books and websites that will provide insights into the changing views about the Appalachians. May you find the story herein of value.

Acknowledgements

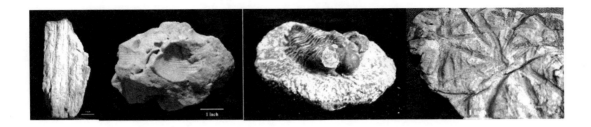

I thank Judith Ann McCarthy, my wife, for her help in putting this together, and for her tolerance and encouragement of my fascination with geology. Susan and Ed Koller, Carolyn and Jack Reeder, Karen Gray, Stephanie Bushong and Margaret King reviewed and suggested improvements. Jim Trott provided some useful references. David Bohaska and Oliver Flint corrected some biological figure captions. Larry Bradford assisted with Civil War history and Roy Pasco assisted with local history references. Many others have helped directly or indirectly with this work, including Amy Elizabeth Melson (including design ideas) and Mary Katherine Melson. Botanist Marion Lobstein took many of us on inspiring and informative fieldtrips in the Fort Valley. Pamela Johnson gave useful tips about design. Friends from the Potomac Appalachian Trail Club, those on Smithsonian Associate Geology Tours arranged by Karen Gray to the Massanutten Mountains and Fort Valley, and the many others who have visited our Geology Study Center have added much to this work in their questions and interest.

Geologists John Haynes, Keith Goggin, Tim O'Hearn, Roger Hubbell and Edward Cotter have been a source of information and enthusiasm during many field trips and conversations about the rocks and geologic history of the Great Appalachian basin. I benefited too from conversations with geologists Richard E. Dovell, at Lord Fairfax Community College, and Richard Perizek, Pennsylvania State University. The aerial photographs in the text were taken during a flight with Geologist-pilot David Diodato over the Fort Valley. This work would not have been possible without all of this generous assistance.

An astronaut took this remarkable photograph (opposite page) from a NASA Shuttle Flight in March, 1994, after a light snowfall. North is at top of the image. The long central ridges are the Massanutten Mountains, and the large valley to the north within them is the Fort Valley. Harrisonburg, Virginia, is just to the left (west) of the southern end of the Massanutten range. To the right (east) of the Range is the valley of the South Fork of the Shenandoah River; to the left (west) is the valley of the North Fork of the Shenandoah River. To the north, the rivers join at Front Royal. The Blue Ridge Mountains extend from the upper right (northeast) to bottom right (southeast) of the image and include much of Shenandoah National Park.[1]

---

[1] Photo courtesy of NASA and the Shuttle astronauts. Available at http://eol.jsc.gov/ Image STS062-104-029.

Figure 1. Fort Valley and Massanutten Mountains from space.

Chapter 1. Introduction

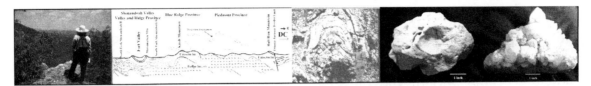

Go my sons and daughters, buy stout shoes, climb the mountains, search the valleys, the deserts, the sea shores, and the deep recesses of the earth...for in this way and in no other will you arrive at a knowledge of the nature and properties of things.

P. Severnius (about 1778)

The Appalachians

The landscapes of the Fort Valley and Massanutten Mountains of Northern Virginia are some of the most beautiful in North America. This book connects these landscapes and their under-lying minerals, rocks, and fossils to the 450 million years or so of Earth history of this part of the Appalachians, one the world's best-known mountain ranges. The area will become our study area, abbreviated FVMM.[2] Both novices and earth scientists unfamiliar with Appalachian geology will find something of interest. For the novice, I have included many of the principles of geology. The area is about 80 miles west of downtown Washington, D.C. and is thus readily accessible for one-day trips. The language of geology is given by definitions in the text and found by the boldfaced terms in the index.

Geology—the study of Earth—depends on field studies. It is based critically on evidence we can see in the field, in the form and constitution of rock outcrops and in the landscape—valleys, mountains, rivers and so forth. These field features are at the heart of geologic appreciation and in our study area include sedimentary rocks, some of them fossil rich, that span from about 450 to 350 million years ago, the lower to middle Paleozoic, the time of ancient life. This was a momentous time because for the first time plants

---

[2] Directions to the area: From the Washington, D.C. area, take Interstate I-66W from the Beltway, to Exit 6 to a left (south on VA-340/522, toward Front Royal) for about a mile, then to a right (west) on VA-55 for 5 miles to Waterlick, then left on VA-678 (the Fort Valley Road), which leads directly into the Fort Valley through the Passage Creek Gorge in the George Washington National Forest. The drive from the D.C. Beltway to the Fort Valley is about 70 miles and takes about 1½ hours.

evolved that could withstand the intense solar radiation and drying necessary for their survival on land. They provided the base of a food chain that led to a great increase in the diversity of land animals of all types, including the first amphibians, our remote ancestors.

In the area is the record of the great Appalachian basin. By including evidence in nearby areas of the Shenandoah Valley and Blue Ridge, we can reconstruct its beginning and its demise in the great mountain building episode at the end of the Permian Period, about 250 million years ago.[3] There is a record too of the motions and rotations of the North America plate that placed it south of the Equator during much of the region's geologic past. Our subject thus covers vast stretches of time, with almost unimaginable landscapes and life forms. It includes times of extreme settings—rising mountains and rapidly deepening seafloors, long-lasting stable settings, shallow seas, marshes, and times of erosion that existed for hundreds of millions of years.

Philip B. King, who studied the Appalachians as well as many areas of the western U.S., wrote a statement that remains true to this day, long after plate tectonics has revolutionized the way in which we think of the Appalachians.[4]

> The Appalachian Chain is the most elegant on earth, so regularly arranged that its belts of formations and structures persist virtually from one end to the other—from its first appearance from beneath the sea in Newfoundland to its final disappearance under the Gulf Coastal Plain in Alabama. What a contrast to the twisted and contorted mountains of middle Europe, or to the confused and superposed rocks and structures in our own western Cordillera! No wonder is it that the Appalachians have been the birthplace of great principles of North American geology and of World geology—to the theory of geosynclines and to theories of folding and faulting, to name only a few. But the apparent simplicity of the Appalachian is deceiving; actually, it is full of guile, and its geology has aroused controversies as acrimonious as any of those in our science.

---

[3] See Chapter 3, p. 47, concerning geologic time.
[4] Philip B. King, *Epilogue* (New York: John Wiley and Sons, 1970). *Studies of Appalachian Geology: Central and Southern.* p. 437.

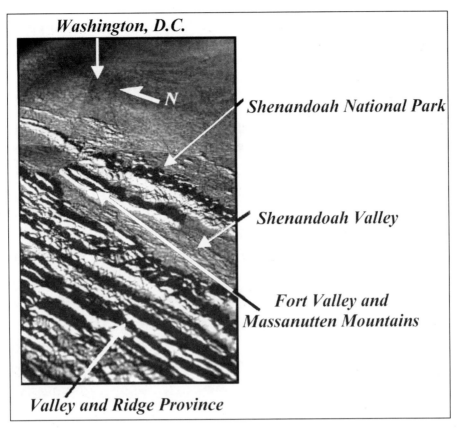

Figure 2. Location of the Fort Valley and Massanutten Mountains.

The area is in the eastern Valley and Ridge province, about five to ten miles west of Shenandoah National Park of the Blue Ridge Mountains (Figure 2, p. 19). It is an isolated mountain belt within the Shenandoah Valley. Photos of the Appalachians taken from NASA's Space Shuttle (Figure 1, p.15) are available on the web and show that the Massanutten Mountains are shaped like a narrow, upside down key ring, or an elongated tuning fork. The Fort Valley—the valley within the valley—fills the northern end of the structure and is typically about five miles wide

The entire range runs 45 miles from its southwest end east of Harrisonburg to its northeast terminus near Waterlick, where US-55 is met by VA-678, the Fort Valley Road. The Massanutten Range splits the Shenandoah Valley in two, creating the valleys of the North and South Forks of the Shenandoah River. A number of peaks in the northern half are well known to hikers: 2500-foot Kennedy Peak overlooking Luray, 2393-foot Meneka Peak, and 2000-foot Signal Knob overlooking Strasburg at the northernmost end (Figure 91,p. 148). The southern portion has its northern end at the New Market Gap and southern end east of Harrisonburg. It is narrow, about 1.5 miles wide, yet has the highest peaks, reaching 3282 feet at Lairds Knob and 2822 feet at Massanutten Peak at the southern end of the Massanutten Mountains.

Approaching the Massanutten Mountains

The Washington, D.C. area is embedded in one of the world's greatest mountain belts. In fact, it is near the core of that belt—which is now recognized as once in the center of the gigantic continent of Pangaea. Thus, we will begin our exploration of the region far to the east, in the Washington D.C. area. Let's go on an imaginary journey that will take us across each of the major zones of this now deeply eroded mountain belt, eventually leading us to the Fort Valley and Massanutten Mountains—in the western part of that same belt. Most of our trip will be on Interstate 66 West and end in our study area, about 65 miles west of the Washington Beltway. Some localities mentioned in the text are marked on the map of Figure 3.

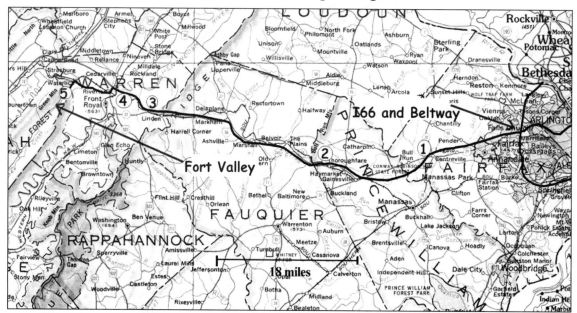

Figure 3. Route from Washington to the Fort Valley. Circled numbers are places mentioned in text between Fort Valley and Washington, D.C. on I-66. **1** *marks the approximate east margin of the maroon sandstone and siltstone of the Leesburg-Culpepper, Triassic-Jurassic basin.* **2** *Thoroughfare Gap, Bull Run Mountain and the Triassic-Jurassic border fault.* **3** *Contact zone of the Blue Ridge Front and Shenandoah Valley ("entrance" to the Appalachian basin proper).* **4** *The Shenandoah Valley, and* **5** *The Passage Creek Gorge—the entrance to the Fort Valley.*

As a geographic matter, the Appalachian Mountains refer to the actual modest mountains of the Blue Ridge, Valley and Ridge, and Allegheny Provinces far to the west. As a geological entity, the Appalachian belt includes not only these but the deformed rocks of the Piedmont province to the east, all unified into a remarkably consistent northeast trend. In Pennsylvania, the Appalachian provinces bend to the east (Figure 6, p. 24), for reasons still debated. The folding of the Valley and Ridge Province ends abruptly along the Allegheny Front, the eastward margin of the Allegheny Province. Although folded, the folds are broad and faulting is far less intense than in the Valley and Ridge Province. Most of the Appalachian coal deposits are in the Pennsylvanian strata of the Allegheny Province.

Beginning at Constitution Avenue in front of the National Museum of Natural History at 10th St., NW, we start on the Coastal Plain, well-hidden beneath buildings and streets (Figure 4). The Coastal Plain consists of the flattish lowlands that extend eastward to the Atlantic shore. One of the finest fossil localities in the U.S. is found in the rapidly eroding cliffs on the central west side of the Chesapeake Bay (Figure 5, p. 22). Beneath the Coastal Plain are the mud, silt, sand, and gravel that are the debris from the erosion of the ancient Appalachian Mountains over millions of years. Entombed in them are fossils including Cretaceous dinosaurs and the teeth of giant Miocene shark found at Scientist's Cliffs (Figure 5, p. 22) and elsewhere on the west side of the Chesapeake Bay.

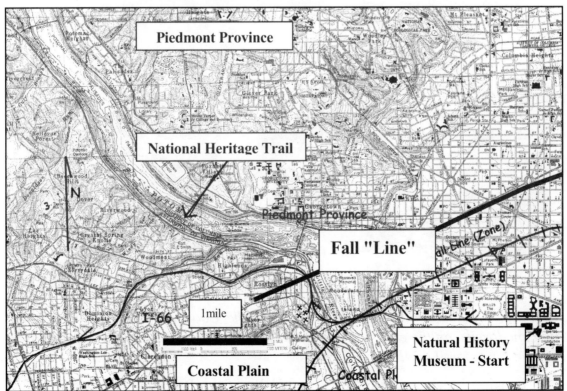

Figure 4. Washington to Arlington—start of the Appalachian crossing.

The Coastal Plain is indeed a vast deposit that extends far beneath the Atlantic onto the Continental Shelf. The eastern end is a zone of great rift faults, left as the Pangaean Mountain Range was broken apart and the Atlantic Ocean Basin took shape. These processes have left us with the western part of the Central Pangean Mountains—the modern Appalachians. We would need to know what's beneath the Coastal Plain and Continental Shelf of eastern North America and the western bulge of Africa and its western shelf to reconstruct the entire Central Pangean Mountain belt. This task is, of course, far from complete and the terrains that are deeply buried beneath the continental shelves may never be well known.

Continuing west on Constitution Avenue, we cross the Roosevelt Bridge and begin a drive that here leaves the Coastal Plain. The next geographic province, the Piedmont, begins just north of the Roosevelt Bridge. The first rocks of the Piedmont are visible in a few outcrops on the shore of Roosevelt Island National Monument and along the National Heritage Trail that starts at Rosslyn and trends northward along the western shore of the Potomac River (Figure 4, p. 21).

Figure 5. Scientist's Cliffs are an outcrop in the Coastal Plain, source of many Miocene fossils, on the east side of the Chesapeake Bay. Clay blocks in right insert contain large fossil scallops.

Erosion in the gorge of the Great Falls of the Potomac (Figure 7, p. 25) has exposed spectacular outcrops of the Piedmont rocks, especially accessible on the Maryland side on Bear Island, just downstream from the

Falls. Here, once deeply buried rocks, some from molten rock (magma) that crystallized into coarsely crystalline granites and other plutonic rocks (igneous rocks that cooled at considerable depth) are beautifully exposed here. The plutonic rocks intruded a wide variety of metamorphic rocks (rocks recrystallized, commonly with the formation of new minerals, in response to high temperatures and pressures) at depth.

The contact between the Coastal Plain and the Piedmont is a zone marked by rapids and waterfalls that limited the navigation of the large ocean-going ships in colonial times. This zone—termed the Fall Line (Figure 4, p. 21)—was thus a port zone, and determined the location of Richmond, Washington (Georgetown), Wilmington, and Philadelphia.

About 20 miles west of D.C., I-66W reaches the maroon sedimentary rocks of the Culpeper Basin that underlie Dulles Airport (Location 1, Figure 3, p. 20). This is one of the many basins formed by rifting and sinking as Pangaea was stretched and broken during its initial breakup in the early Mesozoic (see Geologic Time Scale, Chapter 3, p. 53) when this part of North America was near the Equator. Although dinosaur bones are rare, their footprints are common. Some are beautifully exposed in Dinosaur State Park, a Connecticut basin. Some also are found locally in the Culpeper Basin.

The Culpeper Basin is bounded on the west by a great normal fault (Location 2, Figure 3, p. 20), the east side of which dropped thousands of feet relative to the west side (Figure 8, p. 26). We cross the fault just before the first Appalachian ridge at Thoroughfare Gap through the Bull Run Mountains, a few miles west of VA-15. The Cambrian Weverton Formation, named for Weverton, Maryland, a town near Harpers Ferry, W.Va., is exposed in the cliffs on either side of I-66W in Thoroughfare Gap (just west of Location 2, Figure 3, p. 20). The rock is a quartzite, a metamorphic rock derived by recrystallization here of a quartz sandstone in response to high temperatures and pressures. This happened while the sandstone was deeply buried in the Appalachian Orogen—the term for the entire Appalachian deformed belt.

The Weverton Formation is resistant to erosion and forms the first and easternmost ridge of the vast folded Appalachian Mountains to the west. It underlies the ridge here, and was used to construct the Broad Run Mill, now in ruins. The white cliffs on the west face of Bull Run Mountain south of the Gap are also of the Weverton Formation. These cliffs are more easily viewed from I-66E. The hardness and the ease of splitting into thin slabs have made the quartzite a common flagstone for walks, fences, and the facings of buildings. Concentration of large flakes of white mica derived from clay-rich zones create the easily cleaved beds and are obvious on Weverton flagstone.

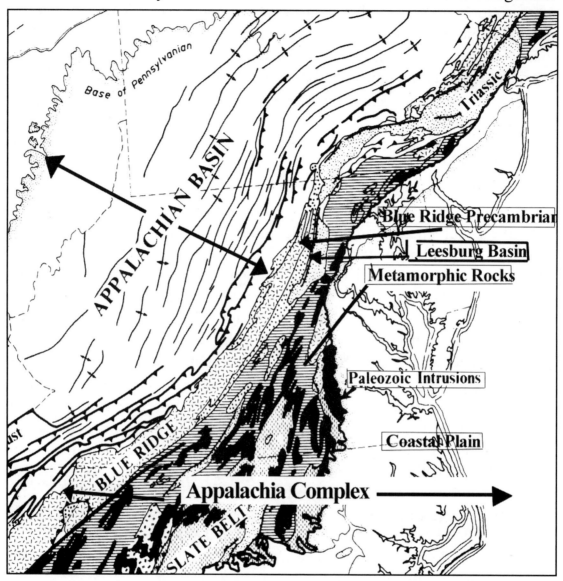

Figure 6. Provinces of the eastern and southern U.S. with major faults and other features of the Appalachian Orogen.[5, 6] The Appalachia Complex and Appalachian Basin have severely folded and faulted, particularly during the Alleghenian orogeny generated by the welding of the bulge of Africa to the eastern part of North America.

[5] After the American Association of Petroleum Geologist's *Tectonic Map of the United States*, 1969.
[6] An orogen is a linear or curved region that has been folded and faulted, and may have a central highly metamorphosed and intruded core (i.e. the Piedmont province of the central Appalachians).

Figure 7. The Great Falls on the Potomac has cut deeply into the rocks of the Piedmont province, viewed from the Maryland side.

Driving through Thoroughfare Gap, the Appalachian mountains surround us as we reach the Markham exit, about 50 miles west of D.C, now far into the Blue Ridge Mountains. In the distance, a prominent ridge with an abrupt northern end—Signal Knob—marks the northwestern end of the Massanutten Mountains. To the south, the ridge rises into a distinct high, Meneka Peak, along Green Mountain, the eastern of the two ridges that cradle the Little Fort Valley (Figure 13, p. 32).

Just past the Linden exit on I-66W, we drive uphill, to the last ridge in the Blue Ridge. As we start down, we see to the left white rocks on a hillside, again of the Weverton formation, here shattered by faulting (Location 3, Figure 3, p. 20). We are crossing the highly faulted zone of the Blue Ridge Front. It is hard to imagine, but the Weverton once extended from Thoroughfare Gap westward in a gigantic arch reaching here, the western edge of the great Blue Ridge-South Mountain anticlinorium (sketched in Figure 8, p. 26). Erosion has cut deeply into this gigantic structure, formed during the final assembly of Pangaea in the Late Permian, about 250 million years ago. Note in the inset in Figure 8 that the beautiful quartzite of the Weverton Formation descends beneath the surface on the west side of this great fold. It never again reaches the surface west of the Blue Ridge Front, and is found only by deep drilling.

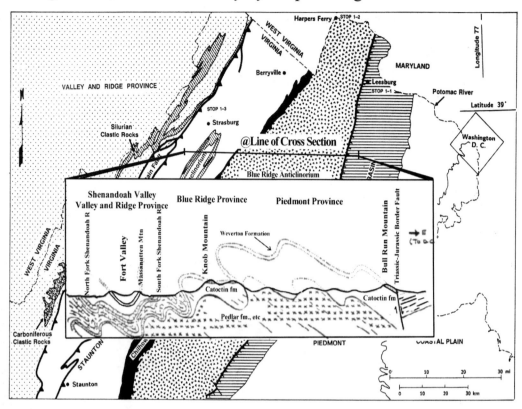

Figure 8. Cross-section along 2nd half of westward trip from Washington close to but south of Interstate 66. Inset is an inferred cross section of the Blue Ridge-South Mountain anticlinorium, and of the Massanutten synclinorium to the west.

Continuing west, we descend into the folded and faulted remnants of the Appalachian basin, leaving the Blue Ridge and entering the Valley and Ridge province. We are now in Cambrian and Ordovician limestone, dolostone, and other sedimentary rocks of the Shenandoah Valley. We exit I-66W at VA-340/55 (Exit 6) just after crossing the Shenandoah River amidst active and abandoned quarries in Ordovician limestone on both sides of the road. The limestone is crushed and used mainly for road gravel (road metal) and for concrete aggregate.

After exiting (I-66W), we turn south (left) for about one mile, crossing the thick shale and siltstones of the seafloor deposits of the Ordovician Martinsburg Formation that are exposed beautifully in road cuts just before crossing the North Fork of the Shenandoah River (Location 4, Figure 3, p. 20). We turn west (right) on VA-55 just after crossing the River. We are now far into the deposits of the ancient Appalachian basin. Here marshes, alluvial plains, tidal flats, and at times an inland sea existed from about 570 to 250 million years ago. As shown in Figure 9, westward flowing rivers deposited great deltas at times stretching hundreds of miles across the basin.

We continue down into the basin and after five miles reach Waterlick. Here we turn south on VA-678, the Fort Valley Road. Rising before us is the north end of the Massanutten Mountains. The mountains shelter the Passage Creek gateway to the Fort Valley (Location 5, Figure 3, p. 20). Our journey has ended, and our story begins.

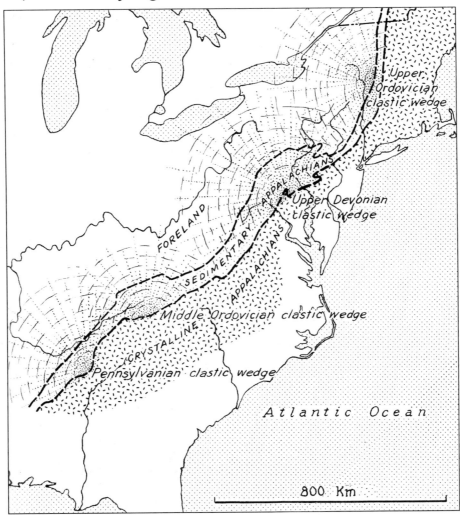

Figure 9. Clastic wedges (deltas near shore) of the Appalachian Paleozoic.[7] Note that the rivers flowed into an interior sea—the great Appalachian Basin. The basin connected the world ocean during much of its 300 million years of existence.

[7] Phillip B. King, *Evolution of North America* (Princeton, N.J: Princeton University Press, 1977), Figure 38, with permission.

The Fort Valley and Massanutten Mountains

All these varied and wonderful processes, by which water mightily alters the earth's surface, have been in operation since the remote antiquity.

Agricola, 1546

The Fort Valley and the enclosing Massanutten Mountains of the George Washington National Forest form a topographic fortress that is widely enjoyed for hiking, biking, horseback riding, and camping. Most of the trails are on the Silurian Massanutten Sandstone once they reach a ridge crest. Table 1 (Chapter 8, p.123) lists the age and rock types of the area, and summarizes some of the major events. Wil Kohlbrenner of the Potomac Appalachian Trail Club (PATC) recently published an extensive guide to the trails of the region.[8]

Northern access to the Massanutten region is by the Fort Valley road (VA-678) that goes south from VA-55 at Waterlick. About 1.6 miles south of Waterlick, VA-678 enters the Passage Creek Gorge that marks the abrupt northern end of the Massanutten Mountains. A number of favorite swimming and fishing spots, including the unusually deep Blue Hole, have been carved by the torrents that periodically fill the gorge. The hard, south-dipping sandstone beds seem to rise up as one moves southward (Figure 10, p. 29). The Massanutten Sandstone forms cliffs and underlies steep talus slopes along the narrow and dangerous curves. These outcrops are our sudden introduction to the Massanutten Sandstone, a formation that is a key to understanding the origin of the Massanutten Mountains. Here, in the Passage Creek Gorge, the formation is a hard, nearly one-thousand-foot-thick barrier to erosion and, more than anything else, is responsible for the impressive cliffs and steep slopes of the gorge.

Suggestions for Additional Information

Some geology journals and books provide a rich source of information on our specific region and on the Appalachians in general. Footnotes provide some of these, and you will find them useful for additional information.

---

[8] Wil Kohlbrenner, *Guide to Massanutten Mountain*, (Potomac Appalachian Trail Club: Vienna, 2000), 116 pp . Kohlbrenner provides information on all official Forest Service trails, some portions of the Tuscarora Trail (formerly the Big Blue Trail), and several undeveloped routes. He also provides some historical information and covers access roads in the Massanutten Mountain sections of the Lee District of the George Washington National Forest. Trails are shown on PATC Maps G and H.

There is also a great deal of information available on the web by simple searches. The Lee District of the George Washington National Forest managed by the U.S. Forest Service also provides a wide variety of information, on everything from campsites to geology.[9] Aerial photographs and maps are available from the U.S. Geological Survey. Important sites to visit include the U.S. Forest Service Massanutten Visitor Center on US-211 at the crest of the New Market Gap. The Gap breaks the northern and southern Massanutten Mountains, and is on outcrops of the Martinsburg Formation.[10]

Figure 10. Silurian Massanutten Sandstone at entrance to the Passage Creek Gorge, dipping southward, at the north end of the Fort Valley.

The Fort Valley Geology Study Center (Figure 11, p. 30) is used for research on Appalachian geology. The PATC's Glass House property borders and overlooks the Study Center from the north. The George Washington National Forest borders the Center on the west, and Passage Creek borders it on the east.[11]

---

[9] The U.S. Forest Service web site URL is www.southernregion.fs.fed.us/gwj/lee

[10] See Table 1, Chapter 8 (p. 123) for description and age of the Martinsburg Formation.

[11] Jewell J. Glass was a PATC member who left her weekend retreat to the PATC. She was a geologist and mineralogist who had worked on many projects for the U.S. Geological Survey, including the Irish Creek tin deposits in the Blue Ridge.

Keith Frye's *Roadside Geology of Virginia* gives much useful information on the geology of all of Virginia.[12] Popular geology publications on adjacent states, such as *The Geology of Pennsylvania*, and Bradford Van Diver's *The Roadside Geology of Pennsylvania* are also good sources of the regional changes in the formations and structures of the Valley and Ridge province described for our study area.[13]

Figure 11. Fort Valley Geology Study Center.[14]

The Forest Service's Story Book Trail, a handicapped-accessible trail exhibiting the region's geology, and ending in a spectacular overlook to the Blue Ridge to the east and southeast, is a short distance north of the Visitor Center on VA-678. Nearby are excellent examples of trace fossils (see p. 105). The Lions Tale Trail is a well-interpreted, handicapped accessible trial. The Forest Service's Pig Iron and Charcoal Trails at Elizabeth Furnace concern 19th century iron smelting. The Hall of Geology, Mineral and Gems in the Smithsonian's National Museum of Natural History in Washington, D.C., is a useful source of information on geology and for viewing spectacular specimens. Also, there are museums on Virginia natural history at Martinsville (geology curator James Beard), at the University of Virginia (Charlottesville), and at Virginia Tech (Blacksburg) with web sites and with geology, rock, or mineral exhibits and some publications.

---

[12] Keith Frye (Missoula, Montana: Mountain Press Publishing Co., 1986)

[13] Charles H. Schultz, editor (Harrisburg, Pa: Geological Survey of Pennsylvania and Pittsburgh, 1999), and Bradford B. Van Diver (Missoula, Montana: Mountain Press Publishing Co., 1990)

[14] Henry and Sam Sager made the modification needed for the Study Center, the wood for the original chicken coup was cut by Claude Ritenour's sawmill, Troy Tamkin wired the building, and architect Andy Boyd did the design.

Figure 12. View looking north toward the State Fish Hatchery from the Buzzard Rock Trail on the north end of Massanutten Mountain. Vista is from near the contact between the Martinsburg Formation and the Massanutten Sandstone. Just south of here, the trail ascends sharply on outcrops of the Massanutten Sandstone.

There are additional sources of information on the regional geology in the literature and on the world-wide web.[15] The Piedmont and Blue Ridge provinces east of the study area include complex faults, rock types, and ages. These exceed the scope of this book and are summarized well on a website by geologist L.S. Fichter of James Madison University.[16] James Dieechio, a geologist at George Mason University, John M. Dennison, University of North Carolina at Chapel Hill, John T. Haynes, University of Connecticut, and Warren Huff, University of Cincinnati, also have work either published or referenced on the web. Web searches will undoubtedly reveal other useful sources of information. In 1989, the Geological Society of America published numerous informative technical papers by some of the most experienced Appalachian geologists.[17]

---

[15] This site is a useful one and has many links: http://www.virginiaplaces.org/geology/index.html

[16] http://csmres.jmu.edu/geollab/Fichter/Fichter/websites.html

[17] R.D. Hatcher, W.A. Thomas, and G. Viele, editors, *The Appalachian-Quachita Orogen in the United States* (Boulder, CO: Geological Society of America, 1989), *The Geology of North America*, Volume F-2.

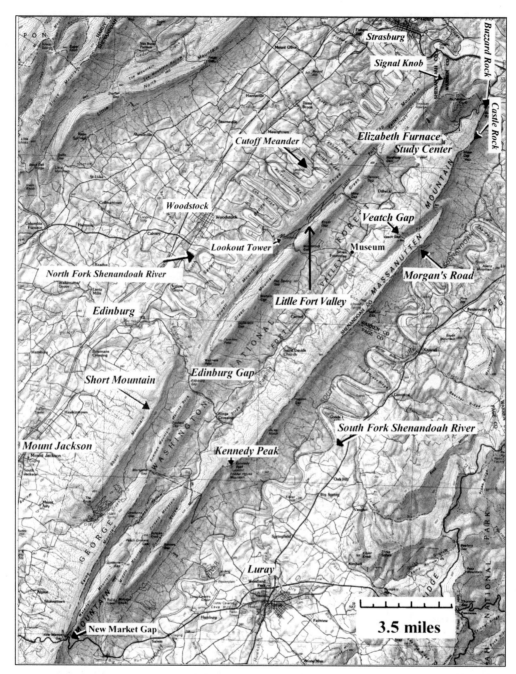

Figure 13. Location of some of the features mentioned in the text in the Fort Valley and northern half of the Massanutten Mountains. The U.S. Forest Service Massanutten Visitor Center at the New Market Gap has exhibits and a good collection of maps and natural history books for sale. Volunteers and rangers there also provide information as to trails and so on.

Chapter 2. History

Most of the early settlers of Shenandoah County came up the Valley from across the Potomac, past Winchester and Middletown. Long before they reached the site of Middletown, they saw the bold headlands of the Massanuttens rising up out of the plain before them and splitting the wide Valley in twain.[18]

–John W. Wayland, 1927

Introduction

The remarkable features of this area have long attracted hikers, naturalists, and, of course, geologists. One of the first geologists to write about it was Arthur Coe Spencer (1871-1964). Robert B. Hoy described Spencer:[19]

> He was born of English parents, September 27, 1871, in Carmel, New York, where both his parents taught in a young ladies seminary; his father music and his mother French. He received his B.S. in metallurgy from the Case School of Applied Science in 1892 and his Ph.D. in geology from Johns Hopkins in 1896 . . . His doctorate thesis described the geology of the Massanutten Mountain, Virginia, a structure in which he never lost interest and in which he revisited many times.

> His experiences in mapping Massanutten Mountain illustrate his self-sufficiency and independence. The country was primitive, undeveloped, and had only a few scattered inhabitants. He would arrange each day's work to arrive at nightfall at a settler's cabin or farmhouse. He always found food and shelter and his hosts must have been amply rewarded by the entertainment of his conversation.

---

[18] J.W. Wayland, *A History of Shenandoah County, Virginia* (Baltimore, Md: Regional Publishing Co., 1980), p. 185 (originally published in 1927).

[19] Robert B. Hoy, *Memorial to Arthur Coe Spencer* (Proceedings of the Geological Society of America for 1966), first quote: page 139, second: p. 140.

Spencer published his study privately in 1895, one which is now hard to find.[20] Work now essential to the geology of the area was done by Eugene Rader and T.H. Biggs (1976) and by Rader and many others (1996).[21,22] These studies provide, respectively, a detailed geologic map of the northern half of the Fort Valley and Massanutten Mountains, and, at less detail, a geologic map of the entire region.

Figure 14. The north end of the Massanutten Mountains, viewed looking south from the Belle Grove Plantation, near Middletown: "the bold headlands of the Massanuttens rising up out of the plain."

Spencer acknowledges at the start the help of Baily Willis, an eminent early Appalachian geologist. Willis's fame derived from an elaborate apparatus that slowly compressed layers of varicolored clay, creating analogs to the magnificent folds of the Appalachian Valley and Ridge province. The Massanutten Mountains are on the eastern part of that

[20] A.C. Spencer, *The geology of the Massanutten Mountain in Virginia* (Washington, D.C: Ph.D. Thesis, Johns Hopkins University, 1895), 54 pp. (private publication) and A.C. Spencer, *A preliminary note on the Massanutten Mountain in Virginia* (Baltimore, Md: Johns Hopkins Circular. 15, 1895), p. 13-14.

[21] E.K. Rader and T.H. Biggs, *Geology of the Strasburg and Toms Brook Quadrangles, Virginia* (Charlottesville, Va: Virginia Division of Mineral Resources, 1976), Report of Investigations 45.

[22] E.K. Rader and others, *Geologic Map of Clarke, Frederick, Page, Shenandoah, and Warren counties, Virginia: Lord Fairfax Planning District* (Charlottesville, Va: Virginia Division of Mineral Resources, 1966).

province, adjacent to the Blue Ridge. Spencer needed this help for he was a student. His book was his doctoral thesis at the Department of Geology, Johns Hopkins University, Baltimore.

Johns Hopkins was then, and for the next century, a center for countless discoveries about the Appalachian Orogen. I feel a kinship with Spencer, for I had studied geology first at Hopkins and then at Princeton, surrounded at both schools by geologists engaged in research on the Appalachians and mountain belts throughout the world. My training in field geology was almost entirely in the Appalachians. My first geologic map was of a portion of the Valley and Ridge province of Maryland near Camp Singewald, the Hopkins Field Camp at that time. It was a difficult and yet exciting project. My doctoral research, though, was in the Rocky Mountains of north central Montana, part of another vast orogen.

Spencer first describes the Shenandoah limestone, a great thickness of limestone, dolomite and other older sedimentary rocks that underlie the Shenandoah Valley outside of the Massanutten Mountains. Spencer considered these the oldest rocks in the area. As geology progressed, the Shenandoah limestone was divided into many formations. They include rocks from the Cambrian and Ordovician Periods, spanning about 130 million years beginning about 570 years ago and ending about 439 million years ago.[23] The Cambrian and Ordovician are the first two of the seven periods of the Paleozoic era, the time of ancient life. Now, as then, a geologic formation is a mappable rock unit. It must have distinctive properties, such as color, texture, fossils, and mineral makeup that allow it to be recognized from surrounding rocks and thus readily outlined on a map.

You may have seen a geologic map with its gaily-colored patterns, but may not have known that each color represents a geologic formation. With a geologic map, we can use the legend to identify the age and rock types upon which we hike or drive, and learn still more in some cases from an accompanying report. Geologic mapping locates formation boundaries, faults, folds, mines, and many other features necessary to reconstruct the geologic history of a region. Geologic mapping also may define new formations, and rename or subdivide old ones. Once a geologic map's symbolism is understood, it reads like a good book, full of intriguing and often mysterious features that sometimes reach far back into earth history.

---

[23] Absolute ages of the geologic periods are from W.B. Harland, R.L. Armstrong, A.V. Cox, L.E. Craig, A.S. Smith, and D.G. Smith, *A geologic time scale 1989*. (Cambridge, G.B: Cambridge University Press, 1990).

To Spencer, and to many geologists who would come later, what some of us call the Massanutten Mountains, were termed the Massanutten Mountain (singular). I stumbled over this seeming error when I first read Spencer's little book. I note, too, that Wil Kohlbrenner in his 2000 trail guide also speaks of the Massanutten Mountain. A myriad of ridges make up the Massanutten Mountains. Many are isolated from one another, such as Short Mountain, located southeast of Woodstock.

But Spencer probably was thinking beyond simple topography. He recognized that all the mountains have two unifying features. First, their crests had outcrops of hard, light-colored rather pure quartz sandstone and quartz-pebble conglomerate of identical properties, those of the Massanutten Sandstone. Second, each ridge was found to be part of a single great fold—a syncline (imagine a smile, see Figure 15)—termed the Massanutten syncline. We speak of it now as the Massanutten *synclinorium*, in reference to the fact that it contains many minor folds, and even anticlines (imagine a frown). In an eroded syncline or synclinorium, the youngest rocks are in the center, the oldest away from the center. Thus, we can conclude immediately and correctly that the shale and other rocks that make up the Fort Valley are younger than the sandstone of the ridge crests.

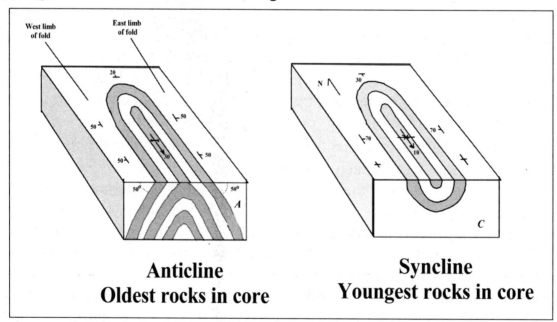

Figure 15. Difference between anticlines and synclines. Both of these folds plunge, or dip, along their axis. For example, the anticline is "plunging" to the south (let north be the far top of each block), the syncline is also plunging to the south. It is thus like the south plunging north end of the Massanutten synclinorium of our study area.

Spencer writes:

> Along the axis of the Shenandoah Valley there is a great
> synclinal fold extending from Staunton, Virginia, to the
> Potomac River, and across Maryland into Pennsylvania. The
> course of this fold is marked by a band of younger rocks lying
> upon the characteristic limestone of the valley.

The Massanutten Mountains and Fort Valley contain the youngest rocks of the Massanutten synclinorium, rocks of the Silurian and Devonian periods. The Devonian period in the Fort Valley is mainly the soft shale, mudstone, and siltstone of the Needmore and Mahantango Formations (see Table 1, p. 123 for description). Marine fossils, especially brachiopod shells, are common in these two formations. Both formations have calcareous layers, and may contain hard calcite-cemented roundish concretions that often are mistaken for dinosaur eggs![24] These formations, however, were deposited millions of years before dinosaurs existed.

E.H. Munch History

The Fort Valley's cultural history began, of course, long before Spencer's visits. E. H. Munch wrote an interesting history of the Fort in 1925, much of it from oral accounts.[25] Here are highlights of his history, some pertaining to geology, geography or archaeology:

(1) The name Massanutten is a native-American word for a basket and refers to the basket-like shape of the ridges that enclose the Valley.

(2) The first European settlers came to the Fort in 1733.

(3) George Washington surveyed the area for Lord Fairfax in 1748 or 1749. Washington noted that the Fort Valley is a natural fortress. During the Revolutionary War, he purportedly assigned Gen. Daniel Morgan of Winchester the task of building a road into the "Fort", a common name still used locally for the Fort Valley. Washington reasoned that the Valley would provide an easily defended fortress should the Continental Army need one. Morgan completed the road into the Fort and it is still there. One of the best places to see the handiwork of the road builders is the buttressing stonework where the trail descends Massanutten Mountain from Veach Gap. It is the road that leads from nowhere and goes to nowhere.

---

[24] The concretions contain the mineral calcite but are mainly made up originally of mud and silt composed of clay minerals, quartz, and other silicate minerals.

[25] See footnote 18, p. 33.

(4) Signal Knob, the northwest terminus of the Massanutten Mountains, was used as a signal post during the Civil War. Signals could be relayed by lanterns near Winchester to Signal Knob and on to Richmond via a number of high mountains of the Blue Ridge. The Civil War Battle of Cedar Creek (October, 1864) was planned from Confederate observations from Signal Knob of the location of Union troops camped around Strasburg.

(5) Three iron furnaces, now in ruins, were operated during the 19th century in the Fort Valley: Elizabeth, Caroline and Boyer furnaces. Munch excludes Catherine Furnace in the southern Massanutten Mountains. Although he writes of remaining rich deposits of iron and manganese, these are small by modern mining standards and because of their irregular shapes are of little commercial value. Other metal deposits are mentioned in the Munch history, including platinum, silver, and gold ores, unlikely ores in association with the rock types that make up the region. An ore by definition is a rock or mineral that can be mined at a profit, that is, they depend on the economic conditions and technology. These change through time. Thus, the past iron ores of the Fort Valley are not ores today: vast iron ores occur elsewhere, as do ores of manganese.

(6) Seven Fountains was a resort that included seven springs.

(7) In regard to wildlife, Munch writes that the last wolf was killed around 1856. The mountain lion also inhabited the area, but also was killed off. Although not mentioned in the Munch history, elk and buffalo also roamed the area (and, I might add, with Passenger Pigeons overhead) before the first European settlement.

Figure 16. Elizabeth Furnace, a 19ᵗʰ century iron furnace, Elizabeth Furnace Picnic Area, George Washington National Forest. Blocks used in its construction are of the Silurian Massanutten Sandstone.

It is appropriate to quote a passage from the Munch history that conveys his feelings about the "Fort":

> Not only is every meadow lined with violets and every hillside dotted with daisies, but the woods are perfumed with the rich and rare fragrance of the honeysuckle and wild crab apple, intersticed with rhododendron, both large and small. Then we come to the glades filled with buttercups and wild rose, and we wonder at the profusion and richness of nature. Again, we wander in the cool refreshing shade of the giant oaks: ponder on their greatness and guess at their age. We try to picture some of the countless scenes of mystery and tragedy that have been enacted under their outstretched branches. Then we look upward toward the blue sky and along the dizzy heights of the cliffs and mountains and see dwarfed oaks and gnarled hardy pines clinging tenaciously to the scant soil in the crevices of the rocks. There the American eagle makes its home; builds it's lofty nest, and rears its young.

Figure 17. Slag, a glass produced as a product of iron smelting, iron ore, and limestone, all part of pig iron production at Elizabeth Furnace. Missing, though, is one essential ingredient: charcoal.

Iron Furnaces

There are four 19th century iron furnaces in the region. Recently, Stanley Dickinson compiled an inventory and description of iron furnaces in Maryland and nearby areas.[26] Elizabeth Furnace, although in ruins, is one of the largest and most accessible in the Fort Valley. Catherine Furnace (Figure 20, p. 42) in the southern Massanutten Mountains on Cub Run is by far the best preserved. Elizabeth Furnace has a remarkable large mass of pig iron on the ground very near the furnace mouth (Figure 18). These furnaces used local iron ore, limestone, and charcoal. Iron ore came mainly from iron oxides in veins, pods, and disseminations in the Ridgely Sandstone, and limestone from one or more of the thin limestone formations just below the Ridgeley Sandstone. Thus, we find each of the furnaces near these deposits. Elizabeth, Caroline, and Catherine furnaces are near the base of the eastern Massanutten ridges, near the first outcrops of these rocks. Moving across the valley, these deposits rise to the surface again, and here we find Boyer Furnace.

---

[26] Stanley K. Dickinson, *A celebration of iron, a history 1609-1802, from Occoquan, VA, to Friendsville, MD* (Baltimore, Maryland: Gateway Press, 2003) contact StanD@frontiernet.net

Figure 18. Large mass of pig iron at Elizabeth Furnace that escaped from its sand mold during the runoff of molten iron from the bottom of the furnace.

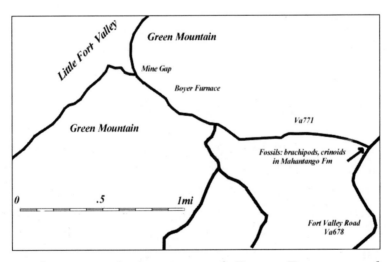

Figure 19. Road map with locations of Boyer Furnace and Mahantango Formation fossil locality.

Figure 20. Catherine Furnace, on Cub Run, southern Massanutten Mountains.

Springs at Seven Fountains

A little can be added to the Munch history concerning the springs at Seven Fountains. Not much is left of a resort that took advantage of the springs in the 19th century, except for some stonework that surrounds some of the springs. Also termed Burner's White Sulphur Springs, it is about one mile east of Detrick on VA-758.[27] Nothing is known about the geological conditions that produce these springs. Typically, springs rise from a permeable layer (an aquifer), such as the Ridgely Formation or one of the limestone formations, as at Elizabeth Furnace.

---

[27] Stan Cohen, *Historic Springs of the Virginias: a pictorial history* (Charleston, West Virginia: Pictorial Histories Publishing Co., 1980), pp. 26-8.

Figure 21. Three-foot high excavated spring near the top of the lower Devonian Carbonate sequence near Elizabeth Furnace that was a possible spa.

There is a possible spa near Elizabeth Furnace (Figure 21). A cut was made that reaches a voluminous spring that is depositing a bright-red iron-oxide rich "slime". Calcite veins in limestone are exposed nearby. The excavation is through the late Silurian to early Devonian limestone sequence. Numerous surface pits just to the north were an important source of iron ore for Elizabeth Furnace.

Figure 22. Fort Valley Museum.

Fort Valley Museum

The Fort Valley Museum (Figure 22) was originally a church built in 1841 and used by many denominations. A small collection of local fossils is amidst many other objects, such as letters, photographs, and clothing. The Museum is one of the few brick buildings in the Fort and was converted to a museum in 1974. A nearby brick house was built of similar brick in 1834. Flood plain deposits on nearby Passage Creek provided the raw material for the bricks.

Figure 23. Hand-axe artifacts from the region.

Lithic Artifacts

Lithic artifacts from the nearby Thunderbird site on the South Fork of the Shenandoah River date back to the about 12,000 years before present. Much younger artifacts from European contact on back occur throughout the region. The dominant rock type used in shaping arrowheads and other tools in the Fort Valley is quartzite from the Massanutten Sandstone. Pottery fragments are uncommon.

Two hand axes from the nearby areas are shown in Figure 23. The right hand axe is from near Harpers Ferry, and is of the Catoctin Formation, a metamorphosed basalt of late Precambrian age (see Chapter 3, p. 53, for the geologic time scale) that is common in the Blue Ridge province east of the Massanutten Mountains. The crude hand axe on the left is from the Shenandoah Valley near Middletown, just north of the northern end of the Massanutten Mountains. It is probably made from quartzite derived from the Massanutten Sandstone. Such materials were just as likely collected from stream cobbles as from outcrops.

Chapter 3. Earth Year and Dating Rocks

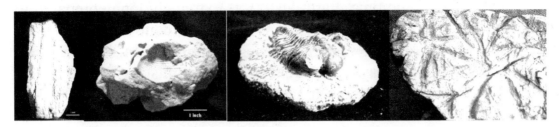

In truth, it is difficult to grasp such an immensity of time because it is so out of kilter with our own brief lifespan. The temptation is to resort to homely metaphors. Imagine the history of the world is represented by a clock face, say, then the appearance of 'blue green' bacteria in the record happened at two o'clock, while invertebrates appeared at 10 o'clock, and mankind, like Cinderella suddenly recalling the end of the Ball, at about one minute to midnight.

Richard Fortey, 1997[28]

Introduction

The age of sedimentary rocks prior to methods of determining the absolute age of rocks was based on relative age: those formations on top of another are younger than those below – the law of superposition. As the relative ages of fossils became established, it was possible to recognize, for example, Ordovician rocks throughout the world if they contained certain key fossils. But how old in years were they, or, what is their absolute age? Thus, a global relative-age stratigraphy was established that lacked an absolute time scale, a quantitative measurement of age.

The youngest folded rocks in the region are still over four hundred million years old. How do we know this? Let's explore this question, for there is nothing more important than to appreciate the immense expanse of geologic time, and how it came to be accurately measured.

---

[28] R. Fortey, *Life: a natural history of the first four billion years of life on earth* (New York: Vintage Books, 1997), p. 16.

An Earth Year

Before examining the method for the absolute dating of rocks, let's examine the vast scale of geologic time. Earth history is extremely long compared to our familiar hours, days, years, and so on. This leads us to speak of "Deep Time" just as we speak of the vast distances in the universe as "Deep Space." We can speak of "Earth Days," and treat all of Earth history as one "Earth Year." If we do this exercise, each Earth Day would equal 4,600,000,000 years (4.6 billion) divided by 365. This gives each of the 365 Earth Days as equal to 12,300,000 years, that is, about 12.3 million years! Humans——*Homo sapiens*——emerged about 100,000 years ago, which would be at 12 minutes before midnight (11:48 pm) on December 31 of our Earth Year. The oldest rock in the Fort Valley—the Martinsburg Formation—is about 460 million years old, or one-tenth of an Earth year, equivalent to November 24. Thus, even 460 million years is but a short time span in Deep Time. The age of the universe is still contested, but values cluster around 15 billion years, and is thought to have been the time of an immense explosion that led to our modern universe.

Radiometric Dating

The discovery of radioactivity was one of the most important in the history of science. It would give evidence for the vast span of geologic time as well as help to determine the fundamental properties of matter. Henri Becquerel (1852 to 1908), a French physicist, discovered radioactivity quite by accident while investigating mineral phosphorescence (the glow induced in some minerals by exposure to visible light or other electromagnetic radiation). Some uranium minerals phosphoresce, and, in the course of his experiments, he found that they emitted penetrating radiation that darkened photographic film. For this work, published in 1897, Becquerel is credited with the discovery of radioactivity. In 1903, he was awarded the Nobel Prize along with Marie and Pierre Curie for the discovery of radioactivity.

Radioactivity plays three important roles in geology. It provides (1) a measure of absolute age, (2) a "tracer" in many geologic systems, and (3) a major source of Earth's internal thermal energy. Thus, natural radioactivity and its consequences are essential to understanding many facets of the physical evolution of Earth, Moon, and meteorites. Radioactivity is the spontaneous change (termed decay) of certain isotopes (atomic varieties of an element) into new ones with the emission of high-energy radiation and/or particles. The high-energy particles include alpha particles (nuclei of helium atoms), neutrons (neutrally charged nuclear particles), and beta particles (electrons). The radiation is typically gamma rays (penetrative, short-wavelength electromagnetic radiation). This is a bare start at understanding the marvelous phenomena of radioactivity.

Radioactive isotopes are in us, in rocks, and even in the atmosphere we breath. Such radiation at these natural levels is minimally harmful. Yet, it can produce some genetic mutation, and thus changes, creating some of the diversity that is needed for natural selection. There is concern, however, about the household accumulation of radon, a radioactive noble gas involved in the decay chain of uranium and thorium. Since radioactive nuclides decay through time, radiation levels were highest during the formation of Earth about 4.6 billions years ago, and still high during the beginnings of life over 3.5 billion years ago.

Zircon, a zirconium silicate, in the Tioga Bentonite (see Table 1, p. 123 for a description of the Tioga Bentonite) is the only mineral that is well suited for radiometric dating in the Fort Valley. It traps readily measurable amounts of thorium and uranium as it crystallizes from molten rock. These two radioactive elements begin to decay, setting the radiometric clock. Zircon from the Tioga Bentonite in the area has, however, yet to be radiometrically dated.

British chemist Ernest Rutherford (1871-1937) and his student Frederick Soddy (1877-1965) discovered in 1902 that the number of atoms of a radioactive element that decay in a given time is directly proportional to the number of radioactive atoms present. This was the beginning of radiometric dating of rocks and minerals. The proportionality constant is termed the decay constant: the larger the decay constant the more rapid the decay. This relationship can be written as: number of new or daughter atoms produced per unit time = a constant number (the decay constant) multiplied by the number of parent radioactive atoms. All other expressions involving age, decay rate, and amount of daughter and parent atoms at any time can be derived from this simple relationship. Only certain isotopes are radioactive, and each radioactive isotope has its own decay scheme. One critical feature of the decay rate is that it is a nuclear process, which means that it is insensitive to pressure, temperature, and the mineral or solution in which the radioactive isotope exists. The rate of decay of radioactive nuclides is commonly expressed as half-life, the time it takes for half of the particular radioactive isotope present to decay. The table on the next page gives the half-lives of radioactive isotopes commonly used for radiometric dating. Those with long half-lives are needed to date very old events.

The first radiometric dates were obtained by Rutherford in 1906 using the amount of helium contained in samples of fergusonite and of a uranium mineral from Glastonbury, Connecticut. He estimated that these minerals had ages of at least 500 million years. This was a profound result, for it directly challenged the biblical notion of a young age for Earth and brought quantitative proof to the subjective evidence of the vast length of geologic time long viewed by geologists, and certainly required by Charles Darwin's views on evolution.

Figure 24. Martinsburg shale, the oldest rock (Ordovician) in the area, near start of the Forest Service Buzzard Rock trailhead parking lot on VA-673, 1.2 miles southeast of its intersection with the Fort Valley Road (VA-678) at about 1.2 miles south of Waterlick.

Because it is a gas, helium might readily escape from a mineral, giving an age that is too low. For this reason, Bertram Boltwood (1870-1927), perhaps the first American radiochemist, used the build-up of lead in uranium minerals as a measure of age. He determined ages between 410 and 2,200 million years on various uranium minerals. Lead is the daughter product of the decay of different isotopes of uranium and thorium that have different half-lives and thus these early methods, long before isotopic

50

measurements were possible, were inaccurate by modern standards. Nonetheless, the very ancient age of some minerals became clear, and represented hundreds and even thousands of millions of years. The vast span of geologic time as revealed unequivocally and verifiably by experimentation using the relentless and constant decay of radioactive atoms is essential in understanding the evolution of the rocks, fossils, and landscapes in the Fort Valley and Massanutten Mountains and of Earth itself.

Isotopes Commonly Used in Radiometric Dating (a=years, ma=millions of years; ba=billions of years)

Parent	Daughter	Half-life	Comments
Carbon-14	Nitrogen-14	5370 y	<50,000 a. Widely used (carbonaceous materials)
Potassium-40	Argon-40	1.25 ba	>0.1 ma. Widely used (potassium-bearing micas, glasses, feldspars)
Samarium-147	Neodymium-147	106 ba	>1 ba. Widely used
Rubidium-87	Strontium-87	47 ba	>100 ma. Widely used
Thorium-232	Lead-208	13.89 ba	>200 ma. Widely used
Uranium-238	Lead-206	4.51 ba	>100 ma. Widely used
Uranium-235	Lead-207	0.713 ba	>100 ma. Widely used

Geologic Time Scale

The story of the Fort Valley and Massanutten Mountains is told in the peculiar language of geology. Particularly hard to remember are the names and sequence of the geologic time scale.[29] The scale is derived from the work of many, many scientists, and has been calibrated by geochronologists —those who date samples based on radioactive decay.

The long-lived isotopes, such as those of uranium and thorium (see above table), are critical to dating minerals that are hundreds of million of years old that is, the truly ancient events in Earth history. Radiocarbon (carbon-14), on the other hand, decays rapidly, and is thus important in dating geologically recent events, such as those of human history.

John McPhee, one of the great popularizers of modern geology, describes a means he used to remember the names of the geologic periods:

> The Paleozoic—544 to 250 million years before the present, a fifteenth of the history of the earth. Cambrian, Ordovician,

---

[29] The ages on time scale are from the 1999 Geological Society of America version.

Silurian, Devonian, Mississippian, Pennsylvanian, Permian. When I was seventeen, I used to accordion pleat those words, mnemonically capturing the vanished worlds of "Cosdmpp," the order of the periods, the sequence of the systems. It was either that or write them in the palm of one hand.[30]

The rocks from the area are from the Silurian, and parts of the Ordovician and Devonian periods. These cover but a small part of all of geologic time (Figure 25, p. 54).

What is the basis on which the sedimentary rocks were broken into geologic periods? One of the most important was the disappearance or appearance of new fossils. Remarkably, the periods have withstood over 100 years of geologic study with but little change, although with the advent of radiometric dating, the boundaries have become more and more precise. How is it that the basic names, though, have survived? The answer lies in that the boundaries reflect fundamental and often global-scale changes.

The discovery of Chicxulub impact crater on the Yucatan Peninsula, Mexico, is a good example of this. The crater was formed by an asteroid or comet which hit the Earth about 65 million years ago, right at the already established boundary between the Mesozoic and Cenozoic eras (the Cretaceous-Tertiary boundary, hence the term K-T boundary for the events timing).[31] The boundary had been recognized because it marked a time of a major biological extinction—more than 50 percent of the Earth's species, including the dinosaurs, became extinct. The crater is between 110 to 180-miles in diameter, and is now buried by 1,000 to 3,000 feet of limestone. It is one of the largest impacts over the past 500 million years or so that have so far been discovered.

---

[30] John McPhee, *Annals of the former world* (New York: Farrar, Straus and Giroux, 1998), p. 83.
[31] The Tertiary Period is the same as the Cenozoic, except it extends up to but does not include the Pleistocene epoch.

Geologic Eons, Eras, and Periods, and their time range, in millions of years[32]

Phanerozoic Eon   *0-570*

Cenozoic Era   0-65   *Recent life*: *Age of the mammals*

Neogene Period	**0-23**
Paleogene Period	**23-65**

Mesozoic Era   65-248   *Middle life: Age of the Dinosaurs*

Cretaceous Period	**65-146**
Jurassic Period	**146-208**
Triassic Period	**208-245**

Paleozoic Era   248-543   *Ancient-life*

Permian Period	**245-290**
Pennsylvanian Period[33]	**290-323**
Mississippian Period	**323-363**
Devonian Period	**363-409**
Silurian Period	**409-439**
Ordovician Period	**439-510**
Cambrian Period	**510-570**

(Precambrian)

Proterozoic Eon	*570-2500*
Archean Eon	*2500-4000*
Priscoan Eon	*>4000*
(Hadean Era)	3800-@4570 (age of Earth)

---

[32]Dates from Harland et al.,1989, *A Geologic Time Scale* (Cambridge, UK, Cambridge Univeristy Press, 1989).

[33]The Pennsylvanian and Mississippian Periods are grouped into the European Carboniferous Period.

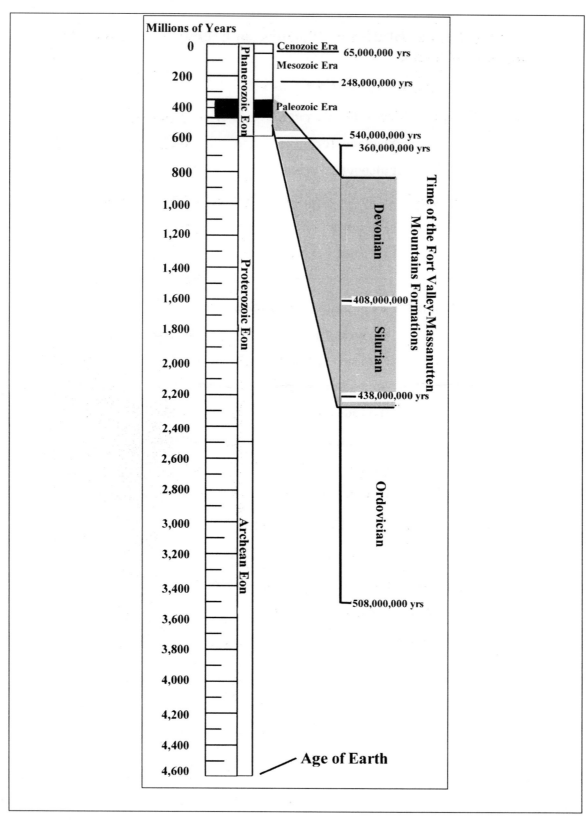

Figure 25. Time span of the strata from the Fort Valley and Massanutten Mountains compared to all of geologic time.

54

Chapter 4. Landscapes

There's nothing constant in the universe,
All ebb and flow, and every shape that's born
Bears in its womb the seeds of change.
 —Ovid, Metamorphoses, V (A.D. 8)

Introduction

The most familiar aspect of Earth is, of course, the landscape. Landscapes are our everyday reminder of Earth's rich history. They may include mountains, valleys, beaches, lakes, or a thousand other forms. Above all, we live on and from their thin veneer of life, soil and water. The landscapes of the Fort Valley and Massanutten Mountain are outstanding. The elegant form of mountains, as if waves upon the sea, is beautifully revealed from space (Figure 1, p.15).

The region is part of the very green temperate climatic zone of the eastern U.S. Its warm colors contrast with the arid barren landscapes of much of the U.S. Southwest. Our rich vegetation springs from moderate temperatures and comparatively high rainfall. Rainfall was particularly high in the year of most of this writing, 2003, reaching 72.88 inches, the highest since 1896, a 108 year-stretch measured at the Leander-McCormick Observatory in Charlottesville, Va. The previous record there was in 1937 (72.07 inches). The 2003 extraordinarily high-rainfall year followed 5 years of severe drought that began in the summer of 1998.

The consequences of the high rainfall were considerable and not all favorable. When hurricane Isabel moved through in mid-September, 2003, many of the largest oaks in the forest on the lower slopes of Green Mountain were uprooted from already soaked and weakened soil. Hurricane Fran brought a similar massive blow-down that selectively uprooted many of the largest of trees in the north end of the Fort Valley, again loosely anchored in water-saturated soil.

Figure 26. Satellite image of Hurricane Isabel at landfall, September 18, 2003, courtesy of NASA.[34] Its impact on erosion and forests in the area were immense.

Erosion

Erosion shapes the land rapidly, geologically speaking. Thus, there are no "old" mountains even though the rocks that underlie them can be hundreds of millions of years old or older, as they are beneath the Massanutten Mountains. The shaping of the landscape is one of the topics of geomorphology, literally the study of the shape of the earth. It deals specifically with present landforms, their origin, description, classification, relationship to underlying structures, and the history of climatic changes.

As erosion wears away the material of the land, Earth's surface rises in response because of the buoyancy of the crust, but always somewhat less than the amount removed. Thus, the surface would still be reduced to a near-sea level, featureless plain (peneplane) in about 50 million years according

---

[34] Courtesy NASA, image at http://science.nasa.gov/headlines/y2003/18sep_isabel.htm

to some estimates.[35] The average erosion rate for Earth's land surface is estimated at about 1 inch in 1000 years, a value that differs greatly, though, from place to place. Arthur Holmes in his classic textbook on physical geology compiled an average global erosion rate throughout geological time of 1 inch per 750 years.[36] One of the highest denudation estimates now is for the arid lands that surround artificial Lake Mead, where the rate is calculated at about 1 inch in 180 years.[37]

In many regions, the surface is rising at rates in excess of the amount removed by erosion. This is clearly required to build mountainous regions and uplifted plateaus, such as the high Colorado Plateau. In our Appalachians, the folding and probable maximum uplift was about 250 million years ago. The uplift, however, did not end then. It appears, instead, that uplift episodically has rebuilt what erosion had worn down. The global erosion rate now is considerably higher than it was during the Paleozoic based on many estimates. The vast shallow inland seas that covered so much of the continents in the Paleozoic and even Mesozoic are now gone.

James Hutton, an English naturalist and a founder of modern geology, wrote in 1785 "The surface of the land is made by nature to decay....our fertile plains are formed from the ruins of mountains." There are two processes that "ruin" mountains: rock weathering and erosion. As we view the ridges and valleys in the Fort Valley and Massanutten Mountains, we are seeing the effects of the work of erosion—the removal of surface materials—mainly by streams and rivers. Denudation is used to describe all those processes that erode the land.

A typical profile of the outer ridges of the Massanutten Mountains is shown in (Figure 29, p. 62). The outer slope is steep, and characterized by cliffs and talus slopes along their base. Beneath is the relatively soft Martinsburg Formation that everywhere surrounds the Massanutten Mountains on their outer slopes. Inside the valley, we find less steep, dip slopes, roughly conforming to the dip of the Massanutten Sandstone (Sm), and leading onto the softer rocks of the Silurian-Devonian limestone sequence (DS).

Let's calculate, albeit roughly, how fast erosion is wearing down the land. Assume that an inch per thousand years holds for the erosion rate of

[35] L.B. Leopold, M.G. Wolman, and J.P. Miller, J.P., *Fluvial processes in geomorphology* (New York: Dover, 1995, paperback republication of 1964 publication), p. 28
[36] From Arthur Holmes, *Principles of Physical Geology* (New York: Ronald Press, 1965), 2nd Edition, p. 516. This remains up-to-date in treating many subjects and does these with excellence.
[37] Above reference, p. 515.

the surface of the Fort Valley. Let's consider its upper reaches, where elevations approach one thousand feet. One thousand feet is twelve thousand inches. At one inch per thousand years, it would take twelve million years to erode the area to near sea level, not allowing for erosional rebound, the rise of the crust in response to removal of the load of the eroded sediment, which we'll explore later when we examine isostasy. As slopes decline, though, the erosion rate will slow.

Nonetheless, geologically, twelve million years is a very short part of the four billion and six hundred million years since Earth's origin. Stated another way, there has been the potential to erode the area to sea level about three hundred and seventy five times! In still another way of looking at this, 4,600,000 inches, or 383,000 feet, or 73 miles of rock, could potentially be removed from the Earth's land areas over the age of Earth. But what's eroded is uplifted again into mountains, only to be eroded yet again. Surely, what we see today did not exist in the distant past nor will it in the distant future. The process of erosion, deposition, and then uplift, and then erosion again, and so on, is termed the rock cycle. Carl Dunbar has stated eloquently the effectiveness of erosion:[38]

> Every feature of the modern landscape was shaped during the last short era of geologic time. The Alps and the Himalayas have come up from the sea floor; the Rocky Mountains have been worn down and then uplifted to their present height; the Appalachians ridges have been etched into relief; and all the other mountain ranges of the world have been elevated and sculptured to their present form since the beginning of the Cenozoic Era.[39]

Glaciation and Mass Wasting

The great continental glaciers stopped far to the north in central Pennsylvania. Thus, our area was not scoured and rapidly eroded as were much of northern Ohio, Pennsylvania, New England, and New York. However, the climate here was quite cold and affected erosion by producing blockfields on the upper slopes of many mountains. The blockfields are, geologically speaking, a recent feature. The Pleistocene Epoch (the time of the Ice Ages) began about 1,640,000 years ago. The slow down-slope creep of boulders and other materials is termed mass wasting and is an important

---

[38] Carl Dunbar, Historical Geology (New York: John Wiley and Sons, 1949), p. 395
[39] The Cenozoic Era began about 65 millions years ago.

agent of erosion. Some large blockfields are precariously balanced near ridge crests and are visible from afar. Large areas of rocks—termed talus—are also accumulating even today beneath sandstone outcrops. Blockfields differ from talus in that they have not been fed by collapse of rocks from an upslope outcrop, and are believed to have formed during the cold climates of the last ice advance. This advance reached its maximum extent about 18,000 years ago.

Blockfields developed by the increased thawing and freezing, which led to fracturing of outcrops, as water in small cracks expands as it freezes, a process termed frost wedging. The intense cold episodes during glacial maximums lowered the tree line, so that the ridge crests of the Massanutten Mountains were barren, and exposed to extreme climates, accelerating fracturing and producing blockfields near and at some places on ridge crests.

A recent pamphlet from the U.S. Geological Survey states that the repeated freezing and thawing shattered bedrock and produced a "jumble" of angular rocks.[40] Blockfields and talus accumulations have three features that are diagnostic of recent movement. First, lichens develop slowly, over tens of years. Thus, blocks that have recently been turned by movement may lack them on one or more surfaces. Secondly, trees may be tilted down slope from recent movements. Their growth then corrects the tilt: again they will grow straight up, creating an upward curving trunk. Finally, tilting and gouging of trunks during an episode of movement may impede tree growth, producing an anomalously thin growth ring. However, this technique requires cutting a tree down to see the growth rings. This goes beyond what the casual naturalist can employ! Blockfields and talus accumulations are an intriguing and unavoidable feature of the ridge crest and near ridge crest trails within the Massanutten Mountains. Blockfields are a reminder of an Ice Age world, quite unlike today. Talus and blockfields are spectacularly developed along portions of the Signal Knob Trail.

Some small valleys that are tributary to Passage Creek have trains of talus of Massanutten Sandstone blocks tens of feet above the central channel. In some cases, these are on both sides of the channel. One good example is along the fire road between Elizabeth Furnace and Mud Hole Gap. They are found above 1000 feet and are possibly the deposits of short-

---

[40] *Geologic Wonders of the George Washington and Jefferson National Forests*, Pamphlet No. 1, Lee Ranger District, produced cooperatively by the U.S. Geological Survey and the U.S. Department of Agriculture, Forest Service, Southern Region, 1998

lived small mountain glaciers. They may be, though, debris flows, and others may be slowly descending talus deposits.

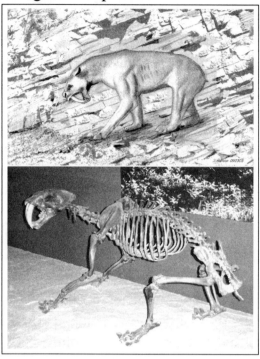

Figure 27. Top: A saber-toothed cat, like those that roamed the Fort Valley during the last glacial advance, around 18,000 years ago. Bottom: Saber-toothed cat excavated from the La Brea Tar Pits, Los Angeles on display in the Ice Age Hall of the Smithsonian's U.S. National Museum of Natural History. The skeleton is about three feet high.

During the last glacial maximum, the plants, animals, and climate differed markedly from today. Huge land-covering glaciers were up to 10,000 feet thick in Pennsylvania. On the seas, the extent of the ice pack and solid ice cover was far more extensive than today. Strikingly, sea level was at least 85 meters lower (279 feet) because of the vast quantities of water frozen into the glaciers. Most of the now submerged continental shelves then were exposed. The grasslands and deserts expanded as forest contracted. Earth became more reflective as light-colored glacial surfaces, grasslands and deserts reflected an immense amount of solar energy back to space (higher albedo) accentuating the cooling compared to today.

Beginning in the Mesozoic ('age of the dinosaurs') and continuing to the present, a wide variety of large reptiles and then, in the Cenozoic, mammals, walked the Fort Valley and Massanutten Mountains. During the last glacial advance, these included mammals such as the saber-toothed cat, shown in Figure 27, that became extinct shortly after this time. The last Ice Age was also a time of other impressively large mammals that are now

60

extinct, such as the mastodon, wooly mammoth, and giant sloth, to mention a few.

Near the end of the last Ice Age, humans, the first paleoindians, reached the new world, and tread our landscapes. Their traces are clear at the Thunderbird Archaeological Site along the South Fork of the Shenandoah River, a short distance east of Massanutten Mountain. Fossils of all of these are rare for there was little deposition that might preserve them. Ice Age mammals have been found, though, in cave deposits in the Valley and Ridge province, but none so far in the Fort Valley.

Floods and Debris Avalanches

All the collected water that flows out of the Fort Valley does so via Passage Creek. This normally sleepy creek became a raging torrent with tremendous erosive force as the remnants of Hurricane Fran passed through in August, 1996. Rainfall was around six inches in the Fort Valley. The Fort Valley road was under several feet of water in many places, and the valley was inaccessible, and remained so for several hours. Passage Creek flooded and damaged the road through the Gorge. There is no record of the amount of material eroded during this storm, but it was surely immense.

Figure 28. Boulders of sandstone on Martinsburg Shale, residual of a prehistoric major flood or a debris avalanche.

However, the destruction could have been much worse. Torrential rains associated with Hurricane Camille loosened rock masses on steep slopes in central Virginia on the night of August 19-20, 1969. By morning, numerous debris avalanches, rapidly moving masses of water-saturated mixtures of soil, trees and rocks, had broken loose and cascaded down slope, leading to fatalities and destruction.

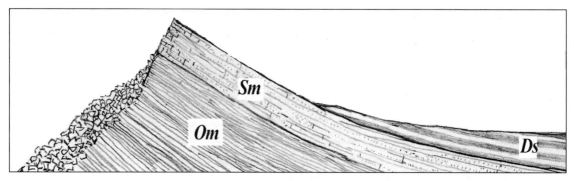

Figure 29. A typical eroded ridge-crest profile controlled by the hardness and dip of the Massanutten Sandstone. Om is the soft Martinsburg Formation, Sm is the hard Massanutten Sandstone and overlying rocks, and DS is the soft limestone and sandstone of the Silurian-Devonian rocks.

To my knowledge, the Fort Valley has not been impacted by debris flows in historic times. Deposits of debris avalanches are common around the outside margin of the mountains (Figure 28, p. 61). There, steep cliffs of the Massanutten Sandstone face outward (Figure 29) and, along with talus accumulations (Figure 31, p. 64), have collapsed and cascaded into the Shenandoah Valley on both the southeast and northwest sides during prehistoric times, probably triggered by torrential rainfall associated with hurricanes or intense rains on thick snow accumulations. The deposits of one or more eroded debris avalanches are crossed by the Buzzard Rock Trail just before it ascends to the top of Massanutten Mountain on the southeast—the South Fork of the Shenandoah Valley side.

The deposits of major prehistoric debris avalanches are also within the Fort Valley. One of the largest and easiest to see is laden with large blocks of the Massanutten Sandstone, and reaches the Elizabeth Furnace Campground. It covers the surface upslope along the Forest Service Road toward Mud Hole Gap and continues westward along the Bear Wallow Trail. Extensive outcrops of the Massanutten Sandstone on the mountainside upstream from the avalanche may be an avalanche scar (source of the avalanche via collapse). The possible scar is clearly visible looking north about a mile up the Bear Wallow Trail. Another collapse from this mountain side would pose a hazard to the campground.

Figure 30. East-facing cliff of the Silurian Shawangunk Formation with an underlying talus slope on the northeast face of Mt. Tammany, on Kittatinny Mountain, Delaware Water Gap, N.J. The Shawangunk Formation is the equivalent of the Massanutten Formation of the study area.

Peneplanes and Uplift

Evidence of episodic uplift may be found in level ridge crests that are similar in elevation. This feature is common throughout the Valley and Ridge province, and beautifully developed in the Massanutten Mountains (Figure 35, p. 68). How might this be explained? One of the oft-cited explanations is that these ridge crests are relicts of an ancient flat, near sea level surface produced by erosion, termed a peneplane. The peneplane was uplifted and the softer shale, limestone and other soft rocks were eroded away from the harder sandstone, leaving the hard sandstone ridges at uniform elevations as the only evidence of the ancient peneplane.

The Schooley peneplane was proposed to be the remnant of a great flat surface dating possibly as far back as 60 million years. This view has been a subject of controversy in the light of an alternate idea proposed by J.T.

Hack. He proposed that the similar ridge elevations are an expected consequence of differential erosion in humid temperate climates.[41]

Figure 31. Talus and outcrops of the Massanutten Sandstone, Passage Creek Gorge.

Differential Erosion

Differential erosion of a folded terrain gives us the elegant topography of the Valley and Ridge province. Erosion refers to the wearing down of the land by water, wind or ice. In arid lands, wind is a powerful force of erosion. Differential erosion means simply that some materials erode more easily than others. For example, the Massanutten Sandstone, which we'll deal with in more detail later, is hard and resistant to erosion. Thus, areas underlain by the hard sandstone are less eroded than the weaker rock strata, mainly, shale that surrounds it (Figure 32, p. 65). Through time, then, the sandstone is left above the general level of the land, as if etched from the surrounding soft rocks. The prominent linear ridges in the Appalachians from Pennsylvania to

[41] J.T. Hack, *Interpretation of erosional topography in humid temperate regions* (American Journal of Science, v. 258-A, 1960) p. 80-97.

Tennessee have the same origin. The Massanutten Sandstone thins to the west, and is equivalent to the Tuscarora Sandstone that underlies many ridges of the eastern Valley and Ridge province.

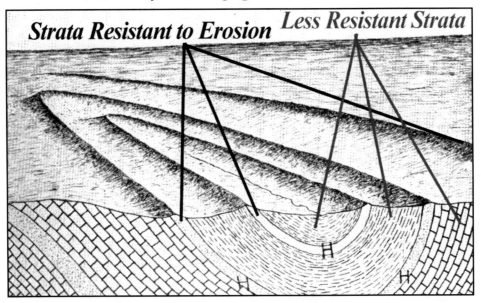

Figure 32. Etching of a terrain by erosion of softer beds of limestone (blocky pattern) and shale (dashed) more rapidly than those of hard sandstone (H, dotted).[42]

Other hard, ridge-forming sandstone and quartzite include, from oldest to youngest and from east to west, the Weverton Sandstone (Cambrian) and Antietam Quartzite (Cambrian), both important ridge-formers in the Blue Ridge province, the Ridgely Formation (Devonian), and the Pottsville Sandstone (Mississippian) of the Valley and Ridge province. The Tuscarora sandstone underlies the spectacular Seneca Rocks of West Virginia, which, like Buzzard Rock, are made up of beds folded to near vertical.

With few exceptions, trails along ridge crests of the eastern Valley and Ridge are on the Tuscarora Sandstone, which correlates with the Massanutten. The Appalachian Trail to the east is on much older rocks, including the Weverton (Cambrian), the Precambrian Catoctin formation (ca. 700 million year old metavolcanic rocks) and the Pedlar formation (1.2 billion year old granitic rock among the oldest rock in the central Appalachians). Without the differences in durability between the hard sandstones and intervening softer sedimentary rocks of the Valley and Ridge province, the region would be topographically rather featureless.

---

[42] Modified from T.C. Chamberlin and R.D. Salisbury, *A college Textbook of geology* (New York: Holt and Co., 1909)

Figure 33. Flood plain, northern Fort Valley along Passage Creek. Massanutten Mountain in background.

Flood Plains

The wide flood plains that border Passage Creek are underlain by fertile soils of clay, silt, sand, and gravel deposited during floods. These provide fields for grazing and farming now and have done so throughout the history of the Valley. A low natural levee, a few feet high, is along the banks of Passage Creek adjacent to flood plains (Figure 33, p. 66). These form during floods in the following way. Floodwaters in the creek move rapidly, and so carry a great deal of sediment, mainly mud and silt. As these spill over into the adjacent flood plains, they eventually back up, causing the flooding waters to slow down, thus depositing some of their load of sediment on the banks, building the levees. The levees are important ecologically for they dam the receding floodwaters. In this way, marshes remain that provide a habitat for a variety of plants and animals.

Figure 34. Gravel and boulders deposited near the Signal Knob Trail parking area, reflecting the ongoing destruction of the mountains by erosion, including sometimes violent, storm-impelled, erosion. Note the size of boulders.

The flood plain materials are in a temporary resting place; some will remobilize and be carried back into Passage Creek during the next great flood. Eventually, they will be carried to the North Fork of the Shenandoah River about one mile northwest of Waterlick, to the Shenandoah River at Front Royal, thence to the Potomac River at Harpers Ferry, and on to the Chesapeake Bay near Point Lookout. Some of the finest particles will settle on the Atlantic continental shelf as the waters of the Chesapeake carry them outward. Only smaller and smaller particles can make this longest journey, coarser ones being left behind.

Figure 35. Flat surfaces of Green and Massanutten Mountains viewed east from the Woodstock Fire Tower on Three-Top Mountain. Looking west from the Fire Tower affords a splendid view of the seven bends of the North Fork (Figure 44, p. 76).

Most of the work of erosion is done during floods. The high velocity of Passage Creek can move boulders and down cut the stream channel (Figure 34, p. 67). The side streams moving down the steep slopes become incredibly powerful erosive forces, moving boulders of the Massanutten Sandstone that are over five feet in diameter.

Meandering Shenandoah Rivers

Rivers typically have bends and these are termed meanders, particularly if they have some regularity to them (Figure 36, p.69). Nowhere in the Appalachians are meanders better developed than along the North and South Forks of the Shenandoah River (Figure 38, p. 71) as they pass just outside the northern reaches of the Massanutten Mountains. Figure 39 (p. 72) shows meanders near the northern end of the North Fork, giving the definitions of wavelength and amplitude as applied to meanders. Meanders erode their outer loops from the tremendous inertia of the water as it turns, extending the outside loop. At the same time, sand bars are deposited on the inner loops, leaving a deposit of sand between each of the growing curves of the meander (Figure 36).

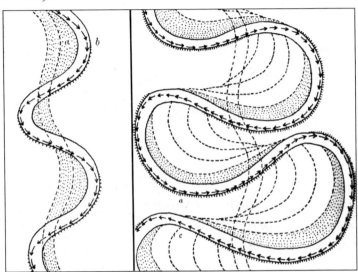

Figure 36. Development of Meanders.[43] *Left figure is an early stage, right, a later stage.*

The reasons for meanders in alluvium (deposits of loose material—mud, silt, sand and/or gravel deposited by streams and their floods) although uncertain, are easy to imagine and experimentally reproducible. However, the cause of those in presumably harder bedrock, as in the case of the two forks of the Shenandoah River, is less clear. Perhaps they developed in alluvium that was deposited during a stage of peneplanation (erosion to a broad flat, possibly near-sea-level alluvium-covered surface). After that, the region underwent broad regional uplift, and the rivers simply continued to erode, following the template of the meanders developed on the much earlier alluvium.[44] On the other hand, they may simply develop in hard rocks as well as in alluvium.[45] The Martinsburg Formation, because it is platy and fractured, may be just as easily eroded as loose sediment.

[43] T.C. Chamberlin and R.D. Salisbury, *A college Textbook of geology* (New York: Holt and Co., 1909), p. 184.
[44] Regional uplift or subsidence is termed epeirogeny (in contrast to orogeny, that involves folding as well as uplift leading to a mountain belt) and is responsible, in an extreme example, for the Colorado Plateau.
[45] For more discussion see footnote 35, p. 57.

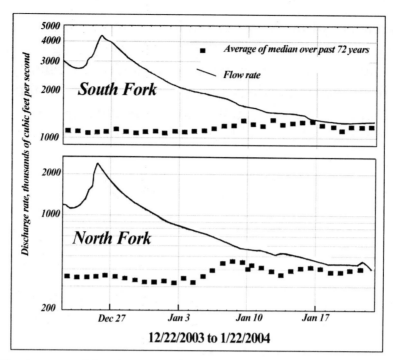

Figure 37. Flow rates of the North and South forks of the Shenandoah River. Data is provisional (subject to correction) from two automatic reporting stations via satellite linkage managed by the U.S. Geological Survey.[46] Note that flow rate (y-axis) has a logarithmic scale. This covers a 31-day period during which there was a storm around December 22, 2003.

But there may be still another explanation about the meanders of the two forks of the Shenandoah as they pass the northern reaches of the Massanutten Mountains. Their entrenchment is entirely in the outcrop belt of the Martinsburg Formation, which is mainly shale and soft sandstone. The meanders turn inward as they reach the limestone that borders the Martinsburg. What causes this distinctive limitation? It may be that the Martinsburg is more easily eroded than the limestone. The limestone also tends to be fractured, but into very large blocks, feet in diameter, and so may erode less easily. On the other hand, limestone is slightly soluble in water, and so might be more easily removed by the river. Yet, it isn't. Thus, I favor the idea that the restriction of the meanders in this area to the Martinsburg is because of the comparative ease of its erosion compared to the limestone.

---

46 USGS site 01634000 North Fork of the Shenandoah River Near Strasburg, VA at http://waterdata.usgs.gov/va/nwis/uv?01634000; USGS site 01631000 South Fork of the Shenandoah River at Front Royal, VA at http://waterdata.usgs.gov/va/nwis/uv?01631000

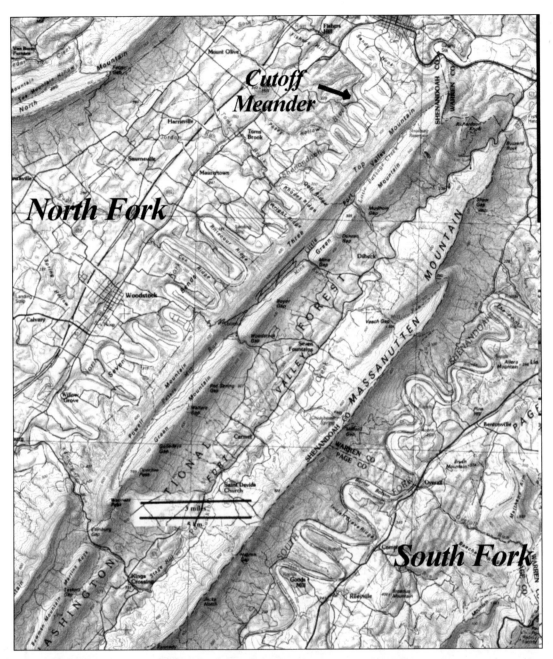

Figure 38. Meanders of the North and South Forks of the Shenandoah River. They become strikingly developed as the rivers flow north and their volumes increase.

The wavelength and amplitude of meanders increase with a river's flow rate. Note that the meander wavelength and amplitude of the South Fork are much greater than those of the North Fork (Figure 37, p. 70). The South Fork's drainage basin is about twice as large (1,642 square miles at Front Royal) as that of the North Fork (768 square miles at Strasburg). Thus, for the storm of early December, and at most times, has a higher flow rate that is around twice that of the North Fork, close to the relative size of their drainage basins.[47]

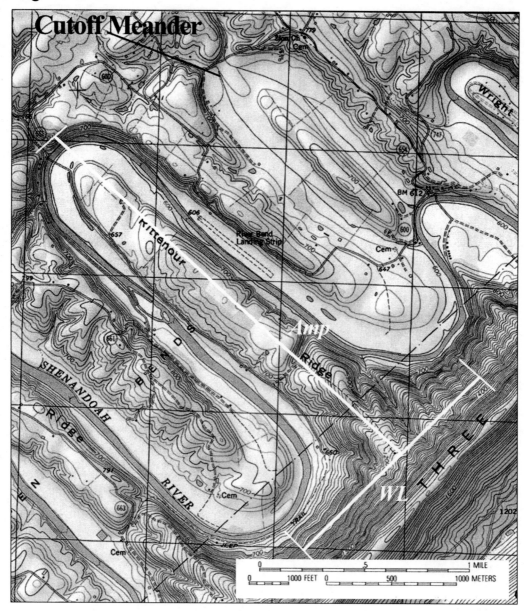

Figure 39. Cut-off meander on the North Fork of the Shenandoah River. Wavelength (WL) and amplitude (Amp) of a meander are defined.

The glacial advance into Pennsylvania diverted water into some rivers. Erosion then cut large amplitude meanders that were later abandoned ('fossil' meanders) as the glaciers retreated. Thus, we find large incised meanders but with small, low flow-rate rivers or streams.

---

[47] see http://www.ccps.virginia.edu/demographics/

Once the North and South Fork merge, the Shenandoah no longer follows the Martinsburg outcrop pattern (Figure 42, p. 74). Instead, it swings far to the east, and hugs the western margin of the Blue Ridge, often flowing entirely on limestone.[48]

Passage Creek has a two bends within its gorge (Figure 43, p. 75) that swing 180 degrees. Here, it is deeply embedded into the hard Massanutten Sandstone. This is strictly speaking not a meander, for meanders ideally are part of a series of bends in a river that are symmetrical, that is, a series of bends that have similar amplitude and wavelength.[49] These two bends may be controlled by weaknesses (easily eroded zones) created by minor folds and faults.

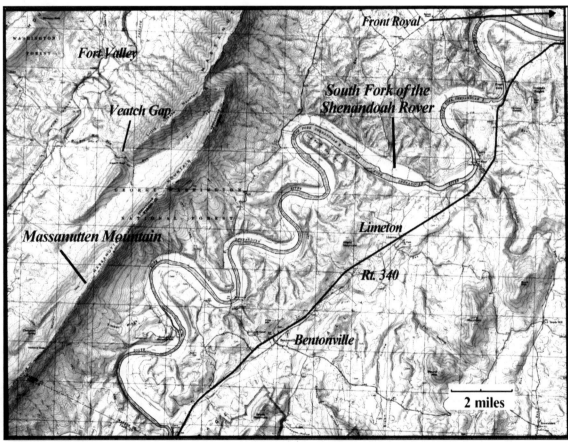

Figure 40. Meanders of the South Fork of the Shenandoah River, southeast of Veach Gap.

---

[48] And dolomite and even Cambrian clastic rocks.
[49] p. 295 in Leopold et al., see footnote 35, p. 57.

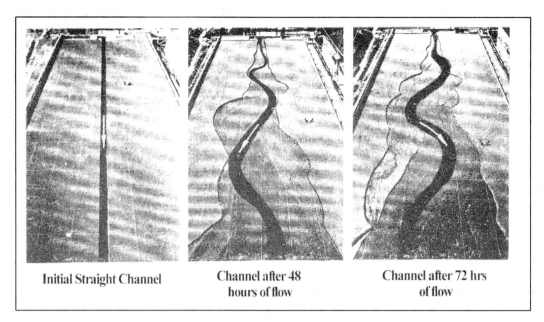

Figure 41. Generation of meanders in Mississippi River sand in an experiment in a 140 foot-long flume. Meanders spontaneously develop after flow is deflected by the first cave in of bank.[50] After 72 hours, a broad valley encloses the well-developed meandering stream. The amplitude of the meanders increases downstream.

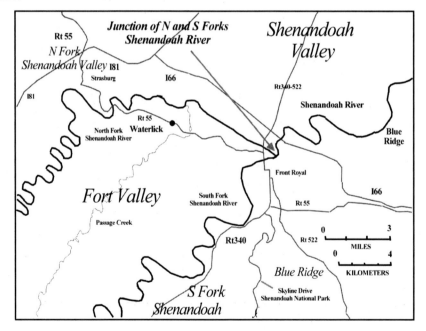

Figure 42. Junction of North and South Forks of Shenandoah River at Front Royal, and eastward course of combined rivers to the Blue Ridge front.

---

[50] J.F. Friedkin, *Laboratory study of meandering alluvial rivers* (Vicksburg, Miss: U.S. Waterways Experiment Station, 1945), plate 2, p. 241

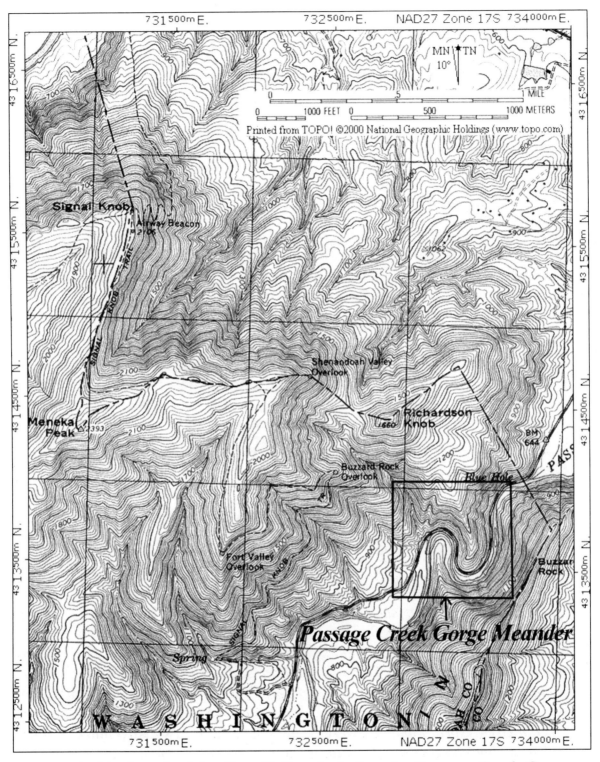

Figure 43. North end of the Fort Valley, including the Passage Creek Gorge. Talus accumulations are on all the steep slopes here. Note the 'meanders' of Passage Creek in box in lower right.

Figure 44. View west from the Woodstock Fire Tower on Three Top Mountain showing one of the Seven Bends of the North Fork of the Shenandoah River. Woodstock is in left (south) middle ground in the Shenandoah Valley, here underlain by Ordovician to Cambrian limestone, dolomite, and shale. The western skyline is Great North Mountain underlain by the Silurian Tuscarora formation. The Massanutten formation beneath Three-Top Mountain and the Tuscarora beneath Great North Mountain were a single layer that was folded into a gigantic arch (anticline) accompanied by faulting and then deep erosion.

Chapter 5. Minerals

A few labeled specimens of minerals and rocks are absolutely indispensable for even a partial understanding of the subject, and students should buy or beg them, if not able to do the better thing—to collect them himself.

James D. Dana, 1895[51]

Introduction

The following four chapters further build the background for the geologic history of our area. They begin with minerals, and move on to rocks and fossils, and end with the formations and their sequence or stratigraphy. Each subject provides unique information about the geologic past, examined in detail in the final chapter.

Minerals in a rock are analogous to the building materials of a house—the wood, bricks, rocks, mortar, and cement. Their arrangement reflects the particular builders and their time. A rock, like a house, contains a detailed record of its origin, revealing more than its individual minerals. Sand and its lithified equivalent, sandstone, illustrate the distinctions between rocks and minerals. Sand and sandstone are especially relevant to the Fort Valley and Massanutten because, as noted above, hard sandstones outcrop along the ridge crests as if holding them up. Most sand grains are composed of quartz, one of the most abundant minerals. As with all minerals, it has (1) a definite chemical composition that can vary only within certain specified limits, (2) specific crystal structure (that is, not amorphous), and (3) is inorganic. The grains of quartz and other minerals reveal the kind of rocks from which our sandstone was derived, and the source rocks are an important part of the story of sandstone.

The specific minerals of the Fort Valley and Massanutten Mountains reveal an interesting story. These minerals are the dominant ones throughout the Valley and Ridge province. There are few rare or unusual minerals.

---

[51] James D. Dana, *The geological story* (New York: American Book Co., 1895), p. 5.

Quartz, calcite, and clay minerals are most abundant. Also, hydrous oxides of iron and manganese are locally abundant enough to have served as ores for the 19th century iron furnaces. Compared to other regions, such as the Blue Ridge and Piedmont provinces, the Fort Valley and Massanutten Mountains have few minerals but these are some of the major ones on Earth.

Most common minerals are silicates, that is, composed mainly of silicon and oxygen, the two most abundant elements of Earth. In these, silicon and oxygen atoms form silicon-oxygen tetrahedra, a silicon atom surrounded by four oxygen atoms at the corners of an equilateral pyramid. The specific structure is given by the way in which these tetrahedra are attached to each other and to other elements, and is the basis for the classification of the silicates and also determines the silicate's physical properties.

Although there are about 3700 minerals, and about 50 new ones are described each year, very few are common. These are termed the rock-forming minerals, and number no more than about 30. Silicates are the dominant rock-forming minerals and determine the physical properties of the solid Earth, except for the Earth's core.[52] A few minor minerals, such as zircon, a zirconium silicate that is commonly used for radiometric dating, and diamond, used in recognition of high pressures, also record important information.

The chemical formula of a silicate mineral (or any compound) is an abbreviation of its composition in terms of atomic amounts expressed as the chemical symbol for each element with a subscript showing the number of atoms in each unit formula. For example, pyrite, fool's gold, is written FeS_2, signifying one iron atom (chemical symbol Fe) for each two sulfur (chemical symbol S) atoms. The absence of a subscript means there is one atom of the element in the chemical formula.

Natural and man-made glass, like obsidian and the slag so common around Elizabeth furnace, are, strictly speaking, not minerals for they have no clear, orderly repetitive atomic structure and can assume a tremendous range in composition. Glass is, nonetheless, abundant in many volcanic rocks and in the products of meteorite impact. Glass is like a frozen liquid, with its atomic components distributed more or less randomly. It forms

---

[52] The core is important even to our story here, for therein derives Earth's magnetic field , a key factor in locating the ancient positions of continents. The core extends out to 3480 km of the 6371 km radius of Earth, and is 32.5% of its total mass (5.975×10^{24} gm). It is divided into a small solid core (1.7% of total mass) in a shell that is mainly molten iron (30.8% of total mass). Thermally driven motions (convection) in the outer core generate electrical and magnetic fields that give Earth its magnetic field.

because atoms randomly arranged in a molten liquid take time to rearrange into the orderly structures of crystals. Thus, most silicate liquids that are cooled quickly by contact with air, water, ice, or a cool rock surface, solidify to glass. The time required for crystallization is largely determined by the composition of the liquid. Some silicate melts, especially those very low in silica, will crystallize so rapidly that they are not found as glass in nature. Other melts, high in silica, like obsidian and the iron-furnace slag, crystallize slowly and so commonly form glasses.

Mohs Hardness Scale

1. **Talc**. Readily scratched by the fingernail, feels soft and greasy.

2. **Gypsum**. Barely scratched by the fingernail. Feels neither greasy nor soft.

3. **Calcite**. Easily scratched by an ordinary steel knife; just scratched by copper, as in a new penny. Most mica, such as muscovite and biotite, has a hardness between 2 and 3. Serpentine minerals are between 2.5 and 3.

4. **Fluorite**. Easily scratched by a knife but not by copper or ordinary glass.

5. **Apatite**. Scratched by a knife and will with difficulty scratch glass.

6. **Orthoclase** (feldspar). Not scratched by a knife and scratches bottle or window glass easily. Most of the other rock-forming feldspars (albite, sanidine, anorthoclase, microcline, and plagioclase) have a hardness around 6. The rock-forming minerals of the pyroxene group are also around 5 to 6.

7. **Quartz**. Scratches a knife and glass easily; harder than other common substances. Olivine also has a hardness of around 7.

8. **Topaz**. Easily scratches quartz.

9. **Corundum**. Scratches topaz and is close in hardness to the manufactured abrasive carborundum. Ruby is a gem variety of corundum.

10. **Diamond**. Easily scratches topaz and corundum with ease. It is the hardest known naturally occurring substance.

Mohs Hardness Scale

The Mohs hardness scale ranks minerals by there relative hardness—the harder can scratch the softer, but not vice versa. It was devised in 1812 by Frederick Mohs, an Austrian mineralogist, and, along with color and crystal shape, remains useful in identifying common minerals.

Mineral Associations

Mineral typically occur with specific other minerals that are stable under similar temperatures and pressure ranges, termed mineral associations. For example, the minerals calcite and quartz, described below, are often found together in sedimentary rocks, for these form at low temperatures. At very high temperatures, such as those of igneous rocks, calcite and quartz decompose, react with one another, yielding carbon dioxide gas and form another mineral association, some containing, for example, wollastonite, a calcium silicate. Thus, knowing one or two minerals in a rock gives clues as to what an unidentified associated mineral might be.

The sedimentary rocks of our study area *a priori* are expected to contain minerals that are stable at low-temperature, such as the clay minerals, and hydrous (water-bearing) iron and manganese oxides. Some minerals, such as garnet, diamond and kyanite, will remain stable far below the high pressure and temperatures of their origin, and can become incorporated in low-temperature deposits, such as sand and gravel.

Figure 45. Milky quartz fills fractures in shattered quartzite float near Elizabeth Furnace. Specimen is about 6 inches long across base.

Quartz

Quartz is by far the most abundant mineral in the area. As just noted, it is the building block of quartzite and most sandstone and one of the most interesting of terrestrial minerals. It is common as minute (millimeter size) but beautiful crystals on fracture surfaces in the Massanutten Sandstone.

Everywhere along ridge-crest trails on the Massanutten Sandstone you will see them sparkle in sunshine.

Figure 46. Quartz crystals from the marine Ridgely (Oriskany) sandstone, from the old Pittsburgh Plate Glass sand quarry just north of Berkley Springs, West Virginia. Quartz crystals are typically six-sided, and capped by a six-sided pyramid.

Quartz is one of a number of crystalline forms assumed by silicon dioxide, composed of one atom of silicon for every two oxygens, written chemically as SiO_2. The simple composition of quartz contrasts with its diverse forms and colors. Rare varieties are tinted purple—amethyst —and some yellow—citrine. In many mines, quartz is one of the main host minerals (gangue minerals) for the ore minerals. Quartz is glassy, transparent, and the hardest common mineral—7 on the Mohs hardness scale—and readily scratches glass. Most rock artifacts found in the area were made from quartzite. The quartz imparts the hardness and suitability for knapping, that is, the flaking (chipping) of a rock into some useful shape, such as an arrowhead or hand axe.

Quartz is made up at the atomic level by silicon-oxygen tetrahedra arranged in a framework, each of the four oxygens of the silicon tetrahedra connect to another external oxygen atom. Brilliant, clear, long six-sided crystals terminating in pyramids are the best-known form of quartz in museums and private mineral collections. More often in nature, it occurs in granular aggregates without the characteristic form. Other crystalline forms of SiO_2 include tridymite, cristobalite, and coesite, a mineral forming only at very high pressure.

Good crystal shapes require growth in sufficient open space that crystals do not meet each other. Such openness is obtained along open fractures (fissures), such as the crystals from a fissure in the Berkeley Springs Quarry, shown in Figure 46 (p. 81). More often, grains are in contact with other grains, preventing the growth of crystal faces and completely filling any open (pore) space, producing in some cases the extremely hard rock quartzite. Regardless of its many forms, all quartz at the molecular scale has the same arrangement of silicon and oxygen atoms.

Quartz is common in many coarsely crystalline light-colored igneous rocks, such as granite. On breakdown of such rock by weathering, quartz is the most resistant, whereas the other minerals, such as the feldspars, decompose. The attack of rain, ground water, and even the corrosive action of plant roots and soil microbes, little affect quartz compared to most minerals. For these reasons, quartz survives as the dominant mineral by far in the beach sands of the Eastern United States, and the ancient beach and river sands of the Appalachian Paleozoic, such as those lithified into the Massanutten Sandstone.

Most but not all the other white-sand beaches of the world are mainly quartz grains. There are, of course, other minerals that are resistant to decomposition by weathering. These are not as abundant as quartz, and include garnet, zircon, tourmaline, monazite, magnetite, ilmenite and many others. Of these, garnet is one of the most abundant on beaches of the eastern U.S., and can give a pinkish tinge to heavy-mineral concentrates on beaches. Concentrations of ilmenite and magnetite give rise to black sands.

In volcanic rocks, silica (another name for silicon dioxide) crystallizes from silica-rich magmas (such as rhyolitic magma) as beta quartz, which on cooling recrystallizes to quartz. Nonetheless, phenocrysts that were once beta quartz retain the elongated (termed prismatic) four-sided crystals capped by four-sided pyramids of what was once beta quartz but are now quartz. Such crystals are said to be pseudomorphs (false forms). Minute quartz crystals formed in this way are in the volcanic ash in the Devonian Tioga Bentonite of the Fort Valley.

Figure 47. Quartz crystals, Arkansas. In the Smithsonian's Museum of Natural History Hall of Geology, Gems, and Minerals.

Calcite

Calcite is the main component of the limestone of the Fort Valley, and occurs in lesser amounts in some of the shale. Although it may form quite attractive crystals, these are dissolved from surface exposures by the high rainfall in the region. Indeed, the many pores in some of the rocks from the Valley were formed by the solution of calcite. This solubility leads to the caves in limestone regions, and accounts for their abundance in the Shenandoah Valley. I know of two small caves in limestone in the northern Fort Valley.

Calcite is composed of calcium carbonate ($CaCO_3$). It is also the dominant mineral in marble, in calcareous sediments, and in the shells of many marine and non-marine invertebrates. In arid and semi-arid lands, it is abundant in soils. Cave formations, many types of deep-sea sediment, and the shells of many organisms are also rich in calcite. Calcite is relatively soft, number three on the Mohs scale, and can be scratched by copper. There are two other crystalline forms of calcium carbonate: aragonite and vaterite. Calcite has a well-developed rhombohedral cleavage, and when an image is viewed through clear crystals or cleavage fragments one sees two images (a phenomena termed double refraction).

Calcite is typically white or colorless, but can occur in colorful forms. It readily bubbles (effervesces) in dilute hydrochloric acid. Field geologists typically have a small bottle of dilute hydrochloric acid (1:5 acid to water) to test for calcite or aragonite. This test also distinguishes calcite from the similar appearing carbonate dolomite, a calcium magnesium carbonate, which does not effervesce in the dilute acid except very weakly in powdered form. Sedimentary rocks rich in dolomite are termed dolostone. Dolomite is also used as a rock name for rocks rich n the mineral dolomite, but the rock name dolostone is preferred for these. Fine-grained sedimentary rocks rich in calcite are termed limestone. Calcite is an important mineral trap for atmospheric carbon dioxide (a greenhouse gas), and thus helps prevent excessive atmospheric temperatures.

Near Elizabeth Furnace, a deep excavation into limestone provides good exposures that include white calcite veins in the limestone found in the bed of a spring that issues from a cave unearthed in the face of the excavation (Figure 21, p. 43). The limestone was mined here as a flux in the iron smelting at Elizabeth Furnace. Conveniently at hand also are a variety of iron-oxide rich rocks that served as ore.

Clay Minerals

Clay minerals are soft and are typically the most abundant minerals in shale, mudstone, soils, and many other materials. They are rich in water, and in many loose aggregates can be shaped and are important in the arts and ceramic industry. Weathering is the main source of the clay minerals. Extremely small particles of clay may be produced on weathering, leading to the abundance on erosion of clay minerals in the finest fraction of marine and other sediments.

Lithification (transformation of soft sediment into rock) tightly binds the clay minerals in shale and mudstone. On weathering, these rocks disintegrate into a residual clay-rich soil. I have tested some of the Fort Valley clays for their suitability for ceramic vessels. Those that formed by weathering of the Needmore Formation (see Table 1, Chapter 8) adjacent to the Geology Study Center are workable and fired nicely at earthenware temperatures to bright orange.

Figure 48. The Needmore Formation (shale) about 5.6 miles south of Waterlick on the Fort Valley Road contains trails (trace fossils) rich in pyrite, now mainly oxidized to orange hydrous iron oxides. Road cut is into the outer bend of a small meander in Passage Creek, which is just off the photo to the right of the road.

Pyrite

Pyrite (iron sulfide, chemical formula FeS_2) is common in small amounts in the shale and mudstone of the Fort Valley.[53,54] I include it here because it played a major role in the origin of the Valley's iron ores, and continues to play an important role in ground water quality, possibly along with the chemically identical mineral marcasite (also FeS_2). In weathered shale and mudstone, there are typically rust-colored spots and trail-like forms colored by hydrous iron oxides derived by the hydration and oxidation of pyrite and/or marcasite. These stains are common in road cuts through the Needmore Formation on VA-678 (Fort Valley Road) just north of the

---

[53] Mudstone is a homogeneous, massive, not platy rock made of lithified mud; shale is lithified mud that breaks into platy fragments (that is, it is fissile). Mudstone and shale are referred to as mudrock.
[54] Where Fe is the symbol for iron and S the symbol for sulfur. The subscript following sulfur symbol indicates there are two sulfur atoms for each iron atom.

Geology Study Center (Figure 48, p. 85). Only on freshly exposed surfaces can the golden (actually brassy) metallic luster of pyrite be seen, properties that gives rise to pyrite's common name of fool's gold. Marcasite has a similar appearance but tends to decompose on weathering even more rapidly than pyrite.

The weathering of the iron sulfides in shale and mudrock produce iron sulfate that dissolves in groundwater and imparts the iron-taste and staining properties of so many Fort Valley wells. It can be removed by appropriate purification systems, but usually at considerable expense. The many clear-water wells in the Valley have tapped ground water that is free of such iron contamination, water that is probably from sand and gravels deposits or from limestone.

The iron sulfides also play a role in the origin of the iron and manganese oxides ores that served the iron furnaces. One model (idea) that may explain this follows. Downward percolation of oxygenated surface water leaches iron and manganese from the Needmore, Marcellus, and Mahantango shale and mudstone. This produces soluble ferrous and ferric sulfates in the groundwater. These sulfates are decomposed into iron oxides in the porous Ridgely Formation. Presumably, manganese behaves similarly. In the Ridgely, basic carbonate-rich waters from the underlying limestone neutralize the acidic metal-bearing sulfate waters. This leads to deposition of the iron and manganese oxides in cavities and fractures in the porous Ridgely.

Iron and Manganese Oxides

Hydrous iron and manganese oxides are in seams, veins, and in the matrix of certain rocks of the Fort Valley. They are typically black, have a brown streak (color of a streak of the mineral scratched across a hard, matt ceramic surface), and are quite dense. The streak test distinguishes them from hematite, which has a distinctive red streak. Some ore fragments are dark brown to black, have a lustrous sheen and botyroidal surface that look like a cluster of grapes. Iron-manganese oxides commonly are found as fern-like coatings (dendritic) on rock surfaces (Figure 49, p. 87). Hydrous iron oxides, such as goethite, are common in the Ridgely Sandstone in small, discontinuous layers and pods, probably formed as discussed above. The iron oxides may contain some manganese and associated manganese oxide minerals. Manganese oxides appear similar to the iron oxides to the naked eye and under the hand lens.

Heavy Minerals in Sand

The Massanutten Mountains and Fort Valley have a rich diversity of mineral grains in sandstone and the sand derived from them. These are the so-called heavy minerals because of their high densities. They resist weathering and erosion and are in small amounts in quartz-rich sand. Finding and seeing them can be a worthwhile challenge. Doing so will take an old fashioned gold pan and some skill at using it. This is because these minerals must be recovered in the heavy mineral fraction of the sands in Passage Creek and similar sites of deposition and concentration. With diligence, red garnet, blue kyanite, doubly or singularly terminated zircon crystals and shiny black crystals of magnetite (which can be pulled out with a magnet) can be found. In some regions of the world (alas, not the sands of our study area), gold is obtained from such heavy mineral concentrates. called placers.

Figure 49. Iron-manganese oxides commonly are deposited in fern-shaped coatings (termed dendrites) on rock surface, and are deposited during weathering. Specimen on exhibit in the Smithsonian's National Museum of Natural History, Hall of Geology, Gems and Minerals.

Chapter 6. Rocks

Sufficient for us is the testimony of things produced in the salt waters and now found again in the high mountains, sometimes far from the sea.

–Leonardo Da Vinci (1452-1519)

Introduction

The study of rocks is termed petrology. The root *petros* refers to rock but petrology is sometimes mistakenly thought to mean the study of petroleum, or "rock oil." Sedimentary, igneous, and metamorphic petrology refer to studies of the three great groups of rocks, all recording different aspects of Earth history. Each rock group provides certain kinds of evidence of origins. Taken together, they are the basis of much of Earth history.[55]

Sedimentary Rocks

Sedimentary rocks are those derived from the deposition of rock fragments or organic material by water, wind, or ice, or of precipitates from water at low temperatures. They are deposited a layer at a time beneath the atmosphere or beneath water or ice. They silently record former dynamic processes involving wind, water, ice, and life. They are divided into two great classes: clastic and non-clastic. The clastic rocks are those derived by deposition of particles (clasts) of pre-existing rocks. In the Fort Valley and Massanutten Mountains, they include mudstone, siltstone, sandstone, and conglomerate. Clasts (pebbles, sand, etc.) are derived by the breakdown of pre-existing rocks. Bioclastic rocks are made up of particles of organisms or produced by organic activity, such as a limestone rich in fossil shell fragments. Limestone and dolomite can bridge the gap between clastic and

---

[55] The detritus layers in drill cores from glaciers and the glacial caps of Greenland and Antarctica also provide unique records of Earth history, including a chronology of temperature change and volcanic eruptions over the last million years.

the second great group of sedimentary rocks, the non-clastic rocks, in that they can contain calcite and dolomite that crystallized directly from water.

The non-clastic rocks also include evaporites, rocks formed by the evaporation of seawater.[56] Our region is composed of rocks deposited beneath the sea (marine rocks) or by the fresh water of rivers or streams (non-marine). Processes within the ancient oceans leave little permanent evidence except for diagnostic features in such rocks.

Figure 50. Quartz-pebble conglomerate in the Devonian Ridgely Formation in the Little Fort Valley near Powell's Fort Camp. Sample is about 18 inches across.

Examples of ancient surface or underwater environments are revealed in any walk through deposits of sedimentary rocks such as beneath the Fort Valley and Massanutten Mountains. Also, and this is of supreme importance, the evidence of ancient life and of our own origins is entombed in sedimentary deposits.

---

[56] Evaporites consist of minerals deposited by the evaporation of seawater. The most abundant of these are gypsum and halite (salt). Although none are present in the Fort Valley, evaporites are common in Silurian sediments, and include the Salina group in New York, long a major source of salt.

Mudcracks in the Silurian Tonoloway formation in a railroad cut at Roundtop, Maryland. These form from the strain of shrinkage as mud dries; common on mudflats in dry climates. Look for them in any dried mud puddle! The Tonoloway formation occurs in the Fort Valley but is poorly exposed.

Figure 51. Mudcracks are evidence of drying of a mudflat, probably one flooded during high tide in the Silurian period. The mud-cracked beds have been folded to nearly vertical from their originally horizontal position.

Lithification and Diagenesis

Sedimentary rocks begin as mud, sand or other such soft materials. How do they become hard rock? This was not clear during the early history of geology and indeed is still controversial for some rock types. In the case of sandstone, the original sand grains have become cemented after burial by interstitial quartz that crystallized from watery solutions usually at low, near-surface temperatures. Calcite may also cement the grains of sandstone. Such post-burial changes, including the change to hard rock (lithification), are collectively termed diagenesis.

Sandstone

Sandstone has a number of important properties useful in reconstructing ancient settings.[57] Of these, current bedding (also termed cross bedding) is one of the most useful for it reveals the directions of flow in the sandstones of the Massanutten formation (Figure 52, p. 93, Figure 53, p. 93, and Figure 54, p. 15). It forms within sand dunes or ripples formed by currents of water or air. Current bedding is evident in sands deposited by waves or by currents in any body of water. It is, fortunately, one of the most common sedimentary structures in the Massanutten Sandstone. Figure 54 (p. 94) shows typical current bedding defined as units of inclined parallel beds that are at an angle to the nearly horizontal beds that bound them.

Clastic sediment and clastic sedimentary rock names are based on grain size[58].	
Sediment (rock)	Grain size
Gravel (Conglomerate)	>2.00 mm
Sand (Sandstone)	>. 0625-2.00 mm
Mud (mudstone)	<. 00006 mm to .0625 mm

L.D. Meckel used cross-bedding to reconstruct the stream directions during deposition of the Massanutten Sandstone. He found that the sands were derived from streams flowing roughly east to west.[59] Also, nearer the source area, conglomerates are common in the Shawungunk formation, the northeastern age equivalent of the Massanutten Sandstone.

---

[57] A sandstone is composed of particles greater than 0.0625 mm and equal to or less than 2.00 mm in diameter.

[58] Udden-Wentworh grain-size scale. Each of these grain-size divisions is divided into many subdivisions. See D.W. Lewis, *Practical sedimentology* (New York: Van Nostrand Reinhold Co. Inc., 1984), see p. 59, for more detail on sedimentary rock classification.

[59] L.D. Meckel, *Alluvial deposition in the central Appalachians: A summary,* in G.W. Fisher, F.J. Pettijohn, J.C. Reed, Jr., and K.N. Weaver, *Studies in Appalachian geology: central and southern* by (New York: Interscience Publishers), pp. 49-67.

Figure 52. Current-bedding in the Shawangunk Formation (Massanutten Sandstone equivalent), Delaware Water Gap, Pennsylvania. Was the current direction from right to left or left to right?

Figure 53. Turtle Rock: record of westward-flowing currents in streams that deposited the sands and gravels of the Lower Silurian Massanutten Sandstone, Story Book Trail, National Forest Service.

Sandstone and Quartzite

The rocks of the Massanutten Sandstone are sometimes called quartzite. What is the difference between a quartz-rich sandstone and quartzite? This is an important question in understanding the origin of the ridges in the Valley and Ridge province. First, in this area a sandstone or quartzite will usually be light-colored, and made of sand grains, which you can see on a natural surface with a hand lens. Examine a broken surface. In a quartzite, fractures go through individual sand grains. In sandstone, the fracture surface wraps around sand grains, and it may even be possible to free sand grains by rubbing the surface.

Figure 54. Current bedding (cross-bedding) in sandstone and current directions (arrow). A is current bedding in the Massanutten Sandstone near Buzzard Rock, and B is from a modern stream deposit displayed in the geology hall of the Smithsonian's National Museum of Natural History, Washington, D.C.

The term quartzite also is used for any rock made up primarily of tightly bound quartz grains. There are two common types. One is derived by tight cementation of quartz sandstone (as in much of the Massanutten Sandstone), the other by the crystallization of quartz in veins from cold to hot watery (hydrothermal) solutions (Figure 46, p. 81). In the Massanutten-Fort Valley area, quartzite of this is type is in veins in the Massanutten Sandstone. Quartzite is also common in the Blue Ridge and Piedmont provinces in veins formed in this way

Shale, Mudstone, and Turbidite

The Martinsburg Formation is composed of thousands of graded beds from inches to over a foot thick. Each cycle consists of a sandstone base that grades upward into mudstone. And this cycle is repeated. Graded beds like these form by deposition from turbidity currents, great submarine avalanches of a slurry of mud, silt and sand. As the avalanche slows down and eventually comes to rest, first sand (now fine-grained sandstone) that grades upward to mud (now mudstone) settles—coarsest first.

A mud rock—a rock made of lithified mud—may be massive (mudstone), or it may easily split into thin plates (shale). Shale and mudstone are common in the Martinsburg Formation.

Louis V. Pirsson and Charles Schuchert, the latter being one of the most incisive of Appalachian stratigraphers, described the process of graded bedding clearly: [60]

> If material of various degrees of fineness be dropped in still water, the heaviest and coarsest particles will descend and reach the bottom first. Upon them will fall the next in size, and so on to the top of the deposit, which will consist of the finest ones, making a regular gradation from bottom to top. [61]

Black Shale

Black shale is the most abundant rock of the Devonian Marcellus Formation. It indicates very specific and interesting conditions in the ancient

---

[60] A stratigrapher is concerned with identifying, naming, and working out the clues to ancient environments provided by sedimentary rocks (the "strata"). Much of their work involves correlating (recognizing time equivalents) over broad regions. Charles Schuchert was a famous Appalachian stratigrapher who did much on this subject in the central and northern Appalachians. A good example of his work is in the paleogeographic maps in the Devonian volumes of the Maryland Geological Survey published in 1909.
[61] L.V. Pirsson, and C. Schuchert, C., *Physical Geology* (New York: Wiley and Sons, Inc., 1924), p. 271

Appalachian sea. Shale is common in the Fort, but most is gray. The peculiar characteristic of black shale is the abundance of dark-colored organic matter. In general, organic matter is oxidized to water and carbon dioxide under conditions of abundant oxygen, as rocks that form in streams and shallow waters, leaving little trace in rocks deposited in such environments.

Therefore, rocks rich in organic matter require very special conditions that prevent oxidation of the organic matter. They include deposition in basins where there is little circulation of oxygenated surface water to the bottom, or accumulation of organic matter at such a high rate that it is not oxidized before it is buried. Once buried under additional organic material, it is isolated from oxygen, and, at high rates of accumulation, will survive. Coal bears testimony to this mechanism. The black shale of the Devonian Marcellus Formation, present throughout much of the Appalachian basin, is exposed in a small roadside quarry about six miles south of Waterlick on the Fort Valley Road as well as small quarries near Seven Fountains.

Conditions that favor deposition for the Marcellus include a very slow influx of mud and silt so that organic matter was an important component of the bottom sediment, and a slow turnover rate of surface to bottom waters preventing aeration. Very warm surface waters have a low density compared to deeper water, impeding surface to bottom turnover and thus creating anoxic (low oxygen) conditions in the bottom sediment. When very little silt and mud reach a basin, the basin is termed a "starved" basin (that is, a basin "starved" for sediment). Evidently, such conditions prevailed over much of the Appalachian sea during this time.

Bentonite and Explosive Volcanism

The sedimentary rocks that underlie the Fort Valley would hardly seem to reflect intense explosive volcanism, yet they contain an unmistakable record of just that in the Tioga Bentonite. Bentonite is a sedimentary rock composed mainly of minute fragments of volcanic minerals and glass, usually in pumice, carried in air from a distant explosive eruption, usually an intense, large volume one. The volcanic rock fragments eventually fell into the sea forming an airfall deposit.[62] The various fragmental products of volcanic eruptions are termed tephra. They typically weather rapidly to clay minerals. There is a great deal of such sediment in the upper part of the Marcellus Shale as well as in the Tioga Bentonite.

---

[62] Pumice is a volcanic rock so rich in gas cavities that it has a density less than one (floats in water).

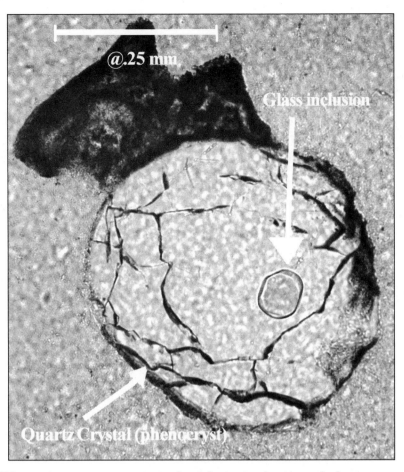

Figure 55. This minute quartz crystal with an inclusion of glass erupted over 300 million years ago as fine volcanic ash that fell into the Devonian sea of the Appalachian basin at that time. This sample is from the Tioga Bentonite near Seven Fountains. The image was taken through a microscope of a polished slice of the rock about one thousandth of an inch thick.

Just as Krakatau, Indonesia, in 1883, left such a deposit in the sea, so too did these eruptions. Ash from the Krakatau eruption reached as far as 6076 km (3776 km), where it fell on the deck of the ship Scotia.[63] The ash is mainly volcanic glass from bubble walls broken into minute fragments. A thick bentonite in a road cut near Seven Fountains contains small quartz crystals derived from beta quartz (Figure 55) with minute inclusions of glass. The glass, although erupted over 300 million years ago, is still as fresh (unaltered) as when it erupted and fell into the sea, protected from alteration by water and organisms by being sealed in the quartz capsule.

[63] T. Simkin and R.S. Fiske, *Krakatau, 1883: the volcanic eruption and its effects* (Washington, D.C: Smithsonian Institution Press, 1983), p. 149.

Volcanic ash (bentonite) layer in the @430 million year-old Ordovician Martinsburg Formation, on Route 340 and 166, just north Front Royal

Figure 56. Geologist Dr. John T. Haynes, expert on bentonite (volcanic airfall ash from distant violent eruptions) in the Appalachian basin: their properties, origin, and significance. Geology Department, University of Connecticut.

Bentonite commonly contains minute crystals of the zirconium silicate zircon. Zircon contains significant amounts of uranium and thorium, as noted in Chapter 3, and so can be radiometrically dated. The date is the time at which the magma that produced the ash began to crystallize zircon, normally close to the time the ash fell into the sea, and thus providing the age of the sediment. Bentonite is thus an especially important sedimentary rock for precisely dating sediments.

Strike and Dip of Rock Structures

After their formation, rocks may be folded, faulted, and fractured. These processes can produce planes that are, for example, faults, where one side has moved relative to the other, or joints, a fracture along which there has been no movement. Originally horizontal or near horizontal layers are produced during accumulation of sediments. These leave planar features, defined, for example, by concentrations of clay particles in sandstone. Such features are termed bedding, and they are commonly the gauge of later faulting and folding. Measurement of the plane's orientation is done in terms of strike (the direction of a horizontal line drawn on the surface) and dip (the tilt of the plane and its direction). This is illustrated in Figure 57.

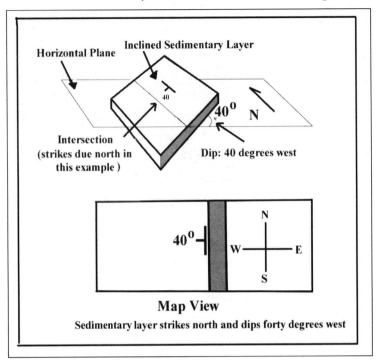

Figure 57. Illustration of the strike and dip of a plane, in this case, a sedimentary layer. Originally horizontal, the layer was tilted 40° to the west. This can happen on the side of an anticline or syncline, or by a fault that dropped the west side of a fault block relative to the east side.

The dip is perpendicular to the strike and measured using an inclinometer, shown in a simplified version in Figure 58 (p.100). The free-swinging needle gives the dip of the plane.

Rock Deformation

Rocks are deformed, for example, during folding. As rocks begin to deform, they first deform elastically, much as a rubber band. Once the deforming forces are released, the rock returns to its original shape. Rocks are, as you might guess, not very elastic. In other words, they can deform only a small amount before one of two things happens: they break (brittle deformation), or deform permanently without fracturing (termed plastic deformation). Figure 59 shows plastic deformation of the seemingly extremely hard rock of the Massanutten Sandstone that produced an anticline. However, note that fractures did develop during folding, as is clear in the figure. We'll return to folds, faults, and other deformation structures in our study area on p. 143.

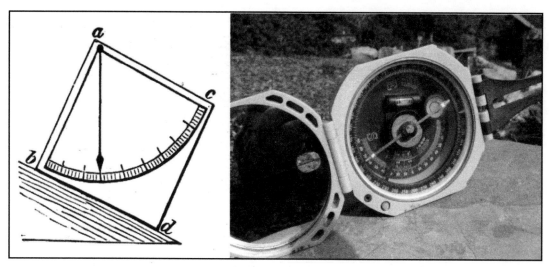

Figure 58. Clinometer (left). A Brunton compass (right) includes a clinometer and compass in the same case.

Figure 59. Anticline in the Massanutten Sandstone. Veach Gap Trail.

Chapter 7. Fossils

> To see the world in a grain of sand,
> And a heaven in a wild flower,
> Hold infinity in the palm of your hand,
> And eternity in an hour.

–William Blake

Introduction

The central Appalachian orogen, viewed as extending from the Allegheny Plateau to the Atlantic coast, preserves life forms spanning about 570 million years, from the Cambrian through Cenozoic time, and is rich in fossil collecting localities. Jasper Burns describes 46 of these, including many in the Valley and Ridge province, but none specifically in our study area.[64,65]

The sedimentary rocks of the Fort Valley and Massanutten contain a wide variety of fossils, some from organisms that lived in or on the sea floor (marine organisms); others, such as those from the Massanutten Sandstone, from fresh water (non-marine) settings, including streams. All the rocks are of Paleozoic age, the time of ancient (paleo-) life. This era begins with the Cambrian Period, a time of a sudden evolutionary increase in the number of invertebrate animals (lacking a backbone) with hard parts and thus readily preserved, such as a variety of shelled organisms, including brachiopods, trilobites, corals, and many others. Plants moved onto the land, and scorpions and insects coevolved with them. After even the youngest of the

---

[64] Jasper Burns, *Fossil Collecting in the Mid-Atlantic States* (Baltimore, Maryland: The Johns Hopkins University Press, 1991), 201 p.

[65] A pamphlet available from the U.S. Geological Survey is also a useful introduction to fossils: L. E. Edwards and John Pojeta, Jr., *Fossils, Rocks, and Time* (Denver: U.S.G.S., Information Services). Go to the U.S.G.S. paleontology web site at http://geology.er.usgs.gov/paleo/ for more information on fossils and geology.

Fort Valley rocks, the Devonian Mahantango Formation (see Table 1, Chapter 8), amphibians evolved from fish, and later still, reptiles evolved from amphibians.

Our oldest fossils are from the Upper Ordovician Martinsburg Formation, the youngest from the Devonian Mahantango Formation. We'll return to these formation names and their meanings in Chapter 8 on stratigraphy. The marine fossils include graptolites, brachiopods, horn corals, trilobites, crinoids, ostracods, and many others. The non-marine fossils are in the Silurian Massanutten formation and include plant impressions and many types of trails left by unknown species of animals on bedding surfaces. Some are vertical tubes that penetrate beds.

Let's trace the appearance of the first vertebrates (chordates), our lineage, with reference to the record of the Paleozoic rocks we have in our study area (Upper Ordovician to Middle Devonian).[66] The oldest fossil vertebrates are found in Upper Cambrian rocks, long before the deposition rocks in the FVMM. These were probably of an armored, jawless fish. Not much is know about these because they are found only as fragments.

During the time of the Martinsburg Formation (Late Ordovician, about 450 million years ago), marine vertebrates diversified into the ancestors of sharks and jawed fish. A number of species of armored jawless fish with sucker-like mouths (ostracoderms) appeared by the mid-Silurian. Some ostracoderms were close to the ancestry of the modern Agnatha—the hagfish and lamprey, others to jawed vertebrates. By then, sediments were deposited in the shallow sea that covered our area, although fish fossils have yet to be found here. The first jawed fish fossils also are found in the Silurian. After our youngest rocks were deposited, the first fossil vertebrates with legs are found in the Late Devonian. Land-dwelling amphibians appeared about 330 million years ago (the Mississippian period). The earliest known ancestor of birds, reptiles, and mammals, are found in early Pennsylvanian rocks, about 300 million years ago, again, much younger than any of the rocks of the Fort Valley.

The fossil descriptions below are a brief summary of the main types of fossils that have so far been found in the area.

---

[66] Chordates (Chodata) are a large phylum of animals that have a rod of flexible tissue) which is protected in later forms (like us) by a vertebral, bony column.

Graptolites

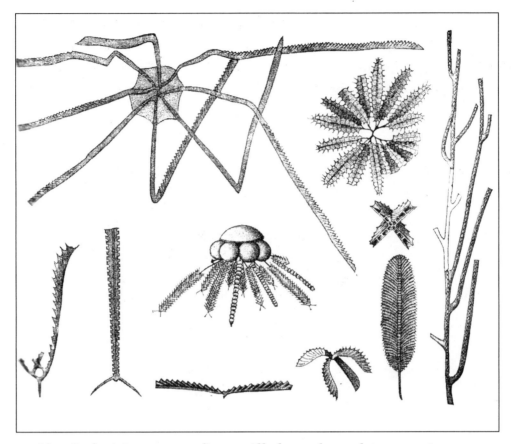

Figure 60. Ordovician graptolites. All less than three centimeters across. Graptolites are found as dark, linear to ornate, delicate thin black films on bedding surfaces of shale.[67]

Patient examination of the platy beds of the Martinsburg can reveal graptolites (Figure 60), organisms that became extinct in the Mississippian Period, so that little is known about their ecology or their relationships to modern organisms. Most were small, marine, free-floating (planktonic) colonial organisms that were extremely abundant in the Ordovician. Nearly identical forms are found in North America, Europe, Australia and elsewhere. Thus, they swan or were carried widely in the world's oceans. For this reason, they are of great use in correlating beds of the same age on different continents. They are, therefore, good index fossils.

---

[67] T.C. Chamberlin and R.D. Salisbury, *A college textbook of geology* (New York: Holt and Co., 1909) p. 531.

Eurypterids

Eurypterids, "sea scorpions", were impressive arthropods and distinctive among Silurian animals. They are first found in Cambrian rocks, became abundant in the Silurian, and declined rapidly afterwards, becoming extinct in the Permian, as part of the greatest extinction in the geologic record.[68]

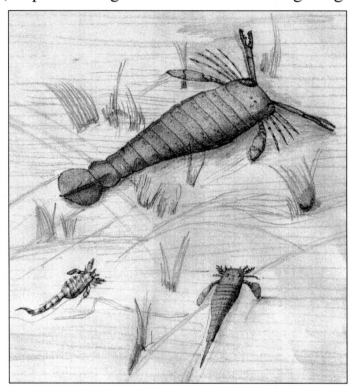

Figure 61. Eurypterids ("sea scorpions") on a Silurian seafloor. The largest is about five feet long and is a reconstruction of Pterygotus buffaloensis from the Silurian rocks of New York State.

Eurypterids are common in some of the Silurian rocks of New York but are, in general, rare. The largest reached over seven feet long with pinchers extended, but most were smaller (Figure 61). Although there are deposits from the Silurian in the Fort Valley, fossils of the bizarre eurypterids have yet to be found. Some may have been able to survive for at least a short time on land. There are impressive reconstructions of Silurian eurypterids and very early land plants in the paleontology exhibits in the Smithsonian's National Museum of Natural History, Hall of Ancient Life (Figure 85, p. 141).

---

[68] Douglas H. Erwin, *The Great Paleozoic Crisis: Life and death in the Permian* (New York, Columbia University Press, 1993*).*

Plant Fossils

Many thin, black-to-dark-gray beds in the Massanutten Sandstone contain black fragments that are some of the oldest known plant remains. Some beds are in the superb exposures in road cuts in the Passage Creek Gorge (Figure 62, p. 105). These plants were a few inches tall at the most, and perhaps like those shown in Figure 85 (p.141).

Figure 62. Channel-fill (filled stream or river) in Massanutten Sandstone (outlined by white lines), Passage Creek Gorge. The impressions of Silurian carbonized plants similar to those are in (Figure 86, p. 105) soft shaly layers between sandstone beds

Trace Fossils

The Massanutten Sandstone contains many trails, tubes, tracks and other markings (trace fossils) left by animals that lived and walked upon the sands of the streams of the Silurian. I have seen at least five different sorts of markings. Such markings without the remains of the animals that made them are termed trace fossils, we have only the traces they left as they moved on or through soft mud or sand. Some of these markings were mistaken for the impressions of plants, and given the name *Arthrophycus alleghaniensis,* such as those in Figure 64 (p.107).

Figure 63. Scolithus, the term for a trace fossil, from the Massanutten Sandstone. B is a side view of A. Such trace fossils are common in the many exposures of the Silurian sandstone along ridge-crest trails.

Some of the best examples of trace fossils in the entire Massanutten Mountains are on the outcrops at the overlook at the end of the Story Book Trail (Figure 66, p. 109). Those with raised ridges (top) show that the creatures moved horizontally in tubes about one inch in diameter just beneath the surface, creating near-surface borings similar to those of the mole or shrew. One immediate alternative explanation of the raised ridges is that they are in reality troughs, requiring that these beds be upside down! It is clear that this is, however, not the case.

Figure 64. Traces left by animals that moved across the soft sand surface of a bed in the Silurian Massanutten Sandstone.

Figure 65. Scolithus verticalis (vertical sand-filled tube) from the Silurian Massanutten Sandstone.

Figure 66. Two types of trace fossils (Scolithus) in the Massanutten Sandstone, Story Book Trail, George Washington National Forest.

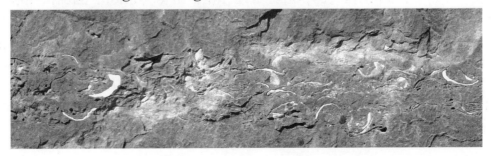

Figure 67. Brachiopods in the Devonian Mahantango Formation in a road cut at the intersection of VA-678 and VA-771 (see map on Figure 19, p. 41). Image is about 6 inches wide.

Brachiopods and Pelecypods

Brachiopods are by far the easiest fossils to find, and were probably the most abundant type of seafloor life that possessed a hard part—their shell. Many, many animals were soft-bodied, and rarely left remains. For example, marine worms and so on, although they may leave tubes or trails on the seafloor, they leave no other record except under extraordinary conditions.

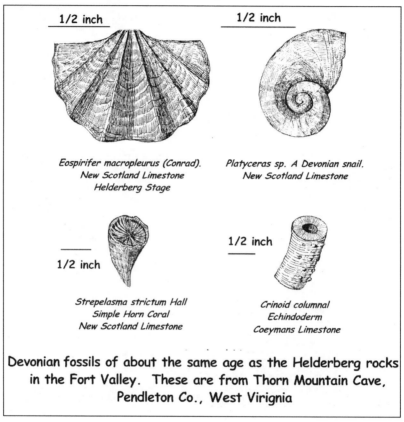

1/2 inch   1/2 inch

Eospirifer macropleurus (Conrad).
New Scotland Limestone
Helderberg Stage

Platyceras sp. A Devonian snail.
New Scotland Limestone

1/2 inch

1/2 inch

Strepelasma strictum Hall
Simple Horn Coral
New Scotland Limestone

Crinoid columnal
Echindoderm
Coeymans Limestone

Devonian fossils of about the same age as the Helderberg rocks
in the Fort Valley. These are from Thorn Mountain Cave,
Pendleton Co., West Virignia

Figure 68. Devonian (Helderberg group) fossils.[69]

Brachiopods and pelecypods have little in common, except that both groups have two connected shells (bivalves), mainly calcareous. The two sides of a shell of a brachiopod are quite different, yet a medial plane perpendicular to the shell line will divide it into two identical parts. Such a plane is termed a plane of symmetry. Pelecypods, on the other hand, have mainly identically shaped shells, that is, the plane of symmetry parallels the shell join.

---

[69]D.R. Lawrence and W.G. Melson, *Geology and Paleontology of Thorn Mountain Cave* (Baltimore, Md: Baltimore Grotto News), v. 3, no. 6, p. 95-97.

Figure 69. Silurian brachiopods in limestone, Fort Valley Road (Va-678) near Elizabeth Furnace.

Figure 70. Brachiopods casts, Devonian Oriskany sandstone (probably equivalent to the non-fossiliferous Ridgely Formation in the Fort Valley), Berkeley Springs Glass Sand Quarry, Berkeley Springs, West Virginia.

Figure 71. Brachiopods from a road cut at the intersection of the Fort Valley Road (VA-678) with VA-771. See map in Figure 19(p. 41) for location. From the calcareous mudstone of the Devonian Mahantango Formation, the youngest Paleozoic formation in the Fort Valley.

Corals

Figure 72. Devonian horn coral, like those found in the Devonian Needmore Formation. These are about 1/2 inch high.

Horn corals are scattered throughout the Needmore as single widely spaced individuals. Horn corals (also called Rugose corals) are solitary organisms that have well-developed septa (the partition between coral polyps). They are first found in Ordovician rocks, and none are found after the Permian. Thus, they became extinct as part of the great Permian extinction.

Trilobites

The race of man shall perish, but the eyes
 Of trilobites eternal be in stone,
And seem to stare about in mild surprise
At the changes greater than they have yet known

–T.A. Conrad

Figure 73. Devonian trilobite, Morocco, about three inches long.

Fragments of trilobites are common in the Mahantango Formation, although common complete individuals (Figure 73 and Figure 74) are rare.

Figure 74. Devonian trilobite, Morocco.

Crinoids

Crinoids (Figure 75, p. 114) are related to the starfish (echinoids) but quite different in that they had a stalk that attached to the seafloor. On death, these stalks disintegrated into numerous circular calcite disks, one of the most common of Paleozoic marine fossils. They are common in the many Fort Valley rocks.

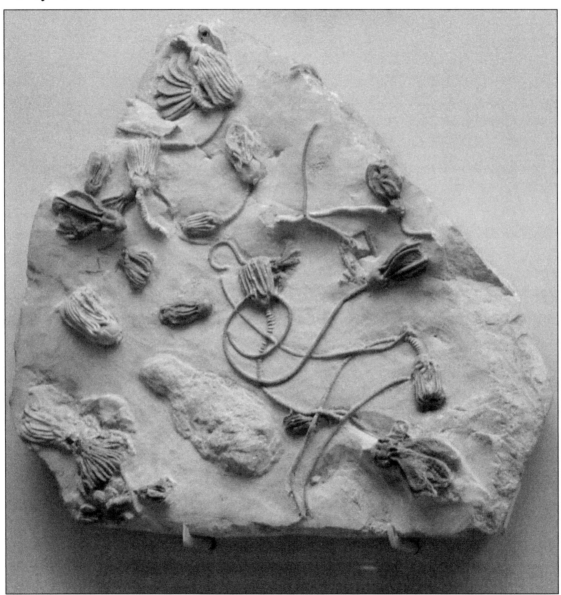

Figure 75. Crinoids on a limestone slab, preserved where they fell on a 380 million year old seafloor. Hall of Ancient Life, Smithsonian's National Museum of Natural History.

Chapter 8. Stratigraphy

Introduction

Like the pages of a book, the layers of sedimentary rocks tell a story. Erosion opens our book of Earth, and we must walk across the landscape to read it. The cover of loose rocks and soil reveal what is happening today. Stream and river incisions, like the surgeon's knife, open for us a profound story. By the time we appear, erosion already has washed away many, many pages and chapters, leaving us to begin to read already deep into Earth history.

Just as minerals are fundamental units in understanding rocks, the formations of stratigraphy are the fundamental units on a larger scale of Earth history. As used here, a sedimentary formation has features that allow it to be distinguished from rocks below and above it. The distinctive properties of the formations in the Fort Valley and Massanutten Mountains and the complete stratigraphy of the area, detailing the events connected with the stratigraphy, are in Table 1 (p. 123).

The terminology of stratigraphy is involved, using such terms as lithostratigraphic unit (the lithology or rock type of strata) and chronostratigraphic unit (referring to age). The distinctions they point to are, however, important. Rocks of similar type can be of quite different age, and rocks of quite different type can be of the same age. Like the unfamiliar terms of geologic time, the terms of the region's stratigraphy can be incomprehensible. Terms like Oriskany, Ridgely, Helderberg, Tuscarora, Mahantango, Marcellus, and so on are familiar terms to Appalachian geologists but not to most others interested in the natural history of the area. Table 1 presents the information necessary to begin to learn these formations. The next step is to examine them in the field.

The Massanutten Mountains and Fort Valley give information about the sedimentary rocks of the east central Appalachian basin—their thickness, fossils, and composition. They are up to 20 miles east of their nearest western equivalents, such as on and west of Great North Mountain near the West Virginia border. They thus provide information for paleogeographic

115

maps, such as the age and location of sea-covered areas, their depth, and the types of organisms that inhabited them far to the east of their main outcrop belt.[70]

Unraveling the mysteries of Earth's distant past depends on our ability to decipher the code of stratigraphy encrypted in the sedimentary rocks. Stratigraphy is key to this task, and focuses on the recognition of distinctive sequences of sedimentary rocks, defining formations, and understanding their origins. It is a fundamental tool in the building of Earth history. At least four methods are used to decipher the significance of sedimentary rocks:

(1) The description of sedimentary sections at various places in the field is an essential part of stratigraphy. This includes the discovery of particularly good exposures that become measured sections. The thickness and properties of the formations are recorded in such sections. Good, well-exposed sections can be rare in areas of few exposures, such as in the Fort Valley. Eugene Rader and Thomas Biggs found and measured such a section, though, in an unnamed tributary of Passage Creek between the Glass House and the Geology Study Center.[71]

(2) Sedimentary petrography involves examining very thin slices (1/1000 if an inch thick) of rocks with a petrographic microscope, and is to geology what histology is to biology.[72,73]

(3) Examination of sedimentation: the processes that form, transport, and deposit sediments in modern times.

(4) Stratigraphy: the overview study of sediments and sedimentary rocks.[74]

The Stratigraphic Record: Lost Pages and Pages Never Written

Two main types of disruptions (unconformities) break the stratigraphic record. The first, a disconformity, is erosion or non-deposition without

---

[70] Construction of Earth's ancient geography- paleogeography- is a major product of geologic research

[71] Described on pages 86-87, in Rader and Biggs (see footnote 21, p. 34). Map coordinates are 15S730010mE, 431062mN at tributary and VA-678 junction; section begins about 300 feet upstream in rough terrain.

[72] Histology is the examination of very thin slices of biological tissue under the microscope.

[73] A petrographic microscope is used to examine thin sections of rocks at very high magnifications, has a rotating stage and polarizer to examine the optical properties of crystals, and has a beneath-stage light source. Modern models include an above stage illuminator that allows polished thin sections to be examined in reflected light.

[74] Sediment usually refers to soft, unlithified materials (sand, gravel, and so on) whereas sedimentary rocks refer to their hard, lithified equivalents.

tilting or folding of the underlying sediments before deposition of the overlying sediment. A disconformity separates the Martinsburg and Massanutten formations. A second type is an angular unconformity, in which folding or faulting and erosion occurred before deposition of the overlying sediment. None of these are in the area.

How much of the record has been removed by erosion of the formations that were once above the Mahantango Formation, the youngest Paleozoic formation in the area? About 20 miles to the northwest there is about 6500 feet of younger Paleozoic formations in Frederick County, Virginia.[75] These include rocks from the Upper Devonian and Mississippian Periods. Much farther to the west, in northwestern West Virginia and southwestern Pennsylvania, there are still younger formations of middle and upper Mississippian, Pennsylvanian and lower Permian age, totaling additional thousands of feet. What may never be known, though, is whether any of these formations extended over the FVMM region before the extensive erosion that began in Permian time and continues today.

Our study area does not include all the formations in Table 1 because of the erosional unconformity between the Martinsburg Formation and the Massanutten Sandstone. Although the Ordovician Oswego and Juniata Formations occur between them to the west in the Toms Brook Quadrangle, they were eroded away before deposition of the Massanutten Sandstone because of uplift connected with the Taconic orogeny, which is discussed more in Chapter 9 (p. 137).[76]

How Are formations Named?

Formation names are derived from the area where the formation was first recognized and described. For example, the Martinsburg Formation was named in 1891 for its outcrop belt just west of Martinsburg, West Virginia, in the northern Shenandoah Valley.[77] The Martinsburg Formation is the oldest in our area and originally was termed the Martinsburg Shale for shale is its dominant rock type, but it contains other rock types as well.

---

[75]C. Butts and R.S. Edmundson, *Geology and Mineral Resources of Frederick County* (Charlottesville, Va: Virginia Division of Mineral Resources, 1966), Bull. 80, p. 14.

[76] Orogeny refers to mountain building, usually involving later compression to form a faulted and folded belt. Usually occurs over periods of millions of years, and, in plate tectonic theory, related to plate convergence, especially of continent convergence involving closing of an oceanic sedimentary basin..

[77] H.R. Geiger and A. Keith, *The structure of the Blue Ridge near Harpers Ferry, Maryland-West Virginia.* (Geological Society of America Bulletin, 1891), v. 2, p. 161.

The most conspicuous formation in our area—the Massanutten Sandstone—was named the Clinch-Tuscarora Sandstone in 1974. The Tuscarora was named after Tuscarora Mountain in Pennsylvania in 1896, and the Clinch from Clinch Mountain, Tennessee, in 1856. This redundancy in names arises because a formation named in one place is eventually identified as identical to one given another name in another area. In the case at hand, the same Silurian sandstone had been given three names: Clinch, Tuscarora, and Massanutten! To the northeast, the same formation has been given still additional names. Normally, the name first used is given precedent. Thus, the name Clinch Sandstone had precedent over the Tuscarora. However, the Tuscarora was so entrenched in the geologic literature that the eminent Appalachian geologist Charles Butts proposed using both names. Butts discusses the origin of most of the FVMM stratigraphic names in his classic book on the "Appalachian Valley".[78]

A Simplified Stratigraphic Column

Figure 76 (p.119) is an attempt to simplify the many and diverse formations described in Table 1. The oldest unit (unit 1, Om) is the lithified marine mud, silt, and sand of the very thick Ordovician Martinsburg Formation. It is followed by a disconformity produced by uplift and erosion (indicated by the wavy line on the top of Ordovician Martinsburg Formation, Om) and then by burial beneath the mainly river and stream sand and gravel of the Silurian Massanutten Sandstone (Unit 2, Sm). The sea again covered the region, this time a shallow sea swarming with life, that deposited limy mud and finally the sand and gravels of streams and possibly of beaches of the late Silurian and early Devonian (Unit 3, Ds). Finally, a thick sequence of fossiliferous Devonian marine mud (Unit 4, Dc), in places with volcanic airfall ash layers, was deposited. Additional interpretations of this stratigraphy are in the final chapter concerning the geologic history (Chapter 9) of the region.

---

[78]Charles Butts, *Geology of the Appalachian Valley in Virginia* (Charlottesville, Va: Virginia Division of Mineral Resources, 1973), Bulletin 52.

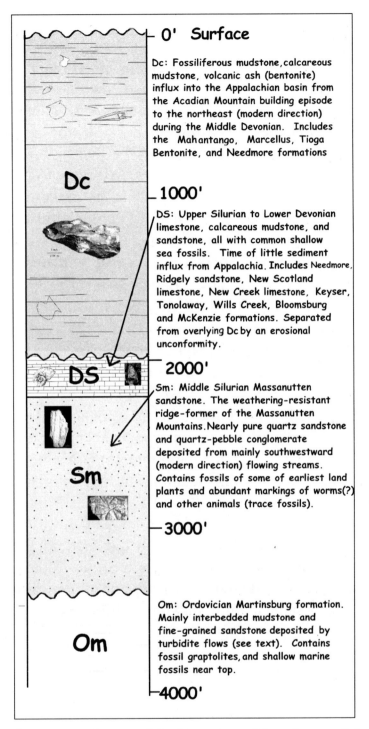

0' Surface

Dc: Fossiliferous mudstone, calcareous mudstone, volcanic ash (bentonite) influx into the Appalachian basin from the Acadian Mountain building episode to the northeast (modern direction) during the Middle Devonian. Includes the Mahantango, Marcellus, Tioga Bentonite, and Needmore formations

Dc

1000'

DS: Upper Silurian to Lower Devonian limestone, calcareous mudstone, and sandstone, all with common shallow sea fossils. Time of little sediment influx from Appalachia. Includes Needmore, Ridgely sandstone, New Scotland limestone, New Creek limestone, Keyser, Tonolaway, Wills Creek, Bloomsburg and McKenzie formations. Separated from overlying Dc by an erosional unconformity.

DS

2000'

Sm: Middle Silurian Massanutten sandstone. The weathering-resistant ridge-former of the Massanutten Mountains. Nearly pure quartz sandstone and quartz-pebble conglomerate deposited from mainly southwestward (modern direction) flowing streams. Contains fossils of some of earliest land plants and abundant markings of worms(?) and other animals (trace fossils).

Sm

3000'

Om: Ordovician Martinsburg formation. Mainly interbedded mudstone and fine-grained sandstone deposited by turbidite flows (see text). Contains fossil graptolites, and shallow marine fossils near top.

Om

4000'

Figure 76. The four units of a simplified stratigraphic column of the formations of the area. Each unit formed under quite different conditions, some beneath the sea, others in streams and flood plains on land. Curvy lines means that there has been erosion after deposition of the underlying formation and before deposition of the overlying formation (a disconformity).

119

Appalachia and the Appalachian basin

The interplay between the Appalachian basin (Figure 9, p. 27) and Appalachia, the landmass to the east (modern direction) explains much of what we see in the rocks of Fort Valley area and throughout the Appalachian Mountains. A great thickness of sediments accumulated in the Appalachian basin—a long, down-warped segment of the Earth's crust. Such great, elongate basins are also termed geosynclines, and seem to be part of a cycle that typically ends in a folded mountain belt, as certainly applies to the Appalachians. Appalachia has been "forged" into its present shape by the various Paleozoic orogenies (Chapter 9, p.125, will describe these), some involving addition of new land areas from converging plates.

The Appalachian basin is now about 1,030 mi (1,657 km) long and about 330 mi (539 km) wide. It covers all of West Virginia and large parts of New York, Pennsylvania, Maryland, Ohio, Kentucky, Virginia, Tennessee, Georgia, and Alabama, and small parts of New Jersey and North Carolina.[79] The basin preserves a wealth of information on life throughout the Paleozoic era.

The volume of sedimentary rocks in the Appalachian basin today, even after millions of years of erosion, is immense, and estimated at about 510,000 cubic miles (2,126,000 cubic kilometers).[80] The bottom of the basin is made up of late Precambrian metamorphic and plutonic rocks. In our study area, the basement is about 30,000 feet beneath the surface. Yet, it reaches the surface where it is has been moved upward along a major Alleghenian thrust fault about four miles to the east along the Blue Ridge Front (Figure 80, p. 135). The eastern margin of the Appalachian basin has the greatest thickness of sedimentary rocks, and is typically highly folded and faulted along this same margin, making it still thicker.

---

[79] G.W. Colton, *The Appalachian basin—Its depositional sequences and their geologic relationships*, p. 5-47 in *Studies in Appalachian Geology: central and southern.* Fisher, Pettijohn, Reed and Weaver, editors. (New York: Wiley and Sons, New York, 1970).
[80] See p. 13 of reference in footnote 79, p. 120.

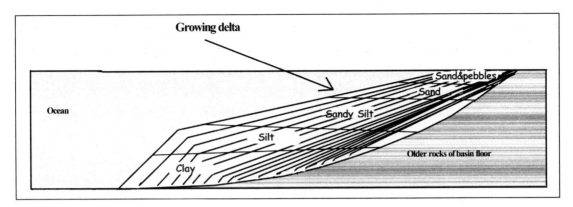

Figure 77. A growing delta illustrates facies change: Horizontal lines mark boundaries between sediment of similar types, but of different age, coarse near shore, fine at a distance. On the other hand, sediment of similar age can be of many rocks types, from pebbles to mud, deposited simultaneously along the delta's surface. This process produces diverse sediment types (lithostratigraphic types) that can be of the same age (chronostratigraphically the same).

Figure 77 shows some of the different sediments deposited in a simplified basin. This figure does not correspond to any particular time but is intended to show and label features that have recurred at many times in the basin's history. Note that in a growing delta, quite different materials were being deposited at the same time—coarse sand and pebbles near shore, and clay far distant. Such a change is termed a facies change. The Massanutten Sandstone becomes coarser to the east and northeast, becoming a conglomerate near Appalachia, its source area. Far to the west, it grades into fine-grained marine sandstone. The Martinsburg Formation provides another example. It grades from a turbidite to a shallow, fossiliferous shelf deposit of shale and sandstone to the south and west, a formation termed the Reedsville.

In 1963 a great simplification was introduced concerning the interpretation of a sequence of sediments, termed sequence stratigraphy, a perspective that recognizes that a sequence of sediments can be related, for example, by the changes expected beneath an advancing sea, starting, in an ideal case, with beach deposits, then shallow water deposits, and then deeper water deposits.[81] Sequences can be broken by major changes in global sea level that leads to erosion.

Seas advanced and retreated across the Appalachian Basin a number of times. Advances of the sea are termed transgressions, retreats, regressions. One example of a transgression occurred after deposition of the non-marine

---

[81] See the geology department at the University of Georgia at www.uga.edu/~strata/sequence site for a detailed explanation of sequence stratigraphy.

Massanutten Sandstone, when the sea moved over the area as recorded by marine fossils in the Bloomsburg Formation. An example of the retreat or regression of sea level happened after deposition of the Martinsburg Formation. Eventually the sea floor rose above sea level, was eroded, and then buried by mainly stream deposits of Massanutten Sandstone time.

Stratigraphic Table

Table 1. Summary of the events, ages, formations and rock types in the Fort Valley-Massanutten Mountains area (abbreviated FVMM in table). Stratigraphic descriptive information has been modified from Rader and Biggs (1976, footnote 21, p. 34)

Age	Name	Properties	Thickness, Ft
		Quaternary: Period of erosion. "Etching" of Valley and Ridge province: hard sandstone and quartzite, such as in the Massanutten and Tuscarora formation and quartzite left higher than surrounding soft, easily eroded rocks, such as shale, limestone, and dolomite. Eroded sediments are deposited on the Coastal Plain and Atlantic Continental Shelf, forming a vast "miogeosynclinal" deposit. A similar environment existed after the breakup of Rodinia and forming of the "ancestral" Atlantic starting about 550± million years million years ago.	
		Continental glaciers of the Quaternary never reached this region; stopping in Pennsylvania.	
		Formation of Atlantic ocean basin. Breakup of Pangaea forming Atlantic ocean, starting about 240 million years ago and continuing today. No deposits in Fort Valley—Massanutten Mountain area (abbreviated FVMM below). Culpeper basin dates from the beginning of this event.	
Quaternary (0 – 1.7 million)	Alluvium	Flood-Plain deposits, fine-grained quartz sand, silt and minor clay and gravel adjacent to streams, mainly along Passage Creek (Figure 33, p. 66).	3-25
		Alluvial-fan deposits of pebbles, cobbles, and boulders of sandstone, quartzite, and conglomerate in a sand matrix, deposited from streams that feed into Passage Creek.	10-30
	Terrace deposits	Pebbles and cobbles of sandstone, quartzite, and conglomerate in a matrix of sand, silt and clay.	0-25±
	Talus deposits	Loose, angular accumulations of cobbles and boulders on steep slopes. Slow down-slope creep of talus is a major process of mountain erosion. Good examples of these are on slopes of the Passage Creek gorge, along the Signal Knob Trail (Figure 31, p. 64).	3-20
	?	Other older deposits of Quaternary - not yet recognized	
		formation of Pangea: Alleghenian orogeny. Major episode of erosion following Permian uplift and folding during Alleghenian orogeny; final convergence of North America and Africa, and formation of Pangaea. Erosion; no deposits in FVMM of this time but the great Massanutten synclinorium and Blue Ridge anticlinorium (Figure 8, p. 26) were folded as were all of the sedimentary formations of the Valley and Ridge province.	
Devonian (363-409 ma)	Mahantango Formation	Greenish-gray, silty shale, siltstone, and very fine-grained sandstone; fossiliferous. All younger formations eroded from FVMM. Exist to the west. Excellent fossil collecting locality at intersection of VA-771 and VA-678 (Figure 19, p. 41 and Figure 67, p. 109)	900+
	Marcellus Shale	Dark-gray to black fissile shale; limestone concretion layer near middle. Excellent outcrops quarried near Seven Fountains	350-400
	Tioga Bentonite	Gray silty shale and siltstone and biotite-bearing, calcareous tuff layers. Volcanic ash layers from tremendous explosive eruptions to east (modern direction). Well-exposed near Seven Fountains. Starts Middle Devonian clastic sequence (mainly mudstone)	80-100
	Needmore Formation	Greenish-gray silty shale and siltstone; fossiliferous. Initiation of increased amount of sediment into the Appalachian Basin from uplift in Appalachia during the **Acadian Orogeny**. Little erosion in the area. Excellent outcrops in road cuts along Rt. 678 about 5.2 miles south of Waterlick (Figure 48, p. 84).	10-450±

	Ridgely Formation	White to gray coarse-grained sandstone and pebbly sandstone, some beds calcareous. Eastern equivalent of the Oriskany sandstone. Not fossiliferous in the Fort Valley. Commonly hematite-rich zones from Quaternary deposition of iron oxides, used in iron smelting.	5-100
	New Scotland Limestone	Dark-gray, silty limestone; gray to white blocky chert; medium- to coarse-grained limestone; fossiliferous. Extremely thin and mainly covered in the FVMM.	10-40
	New Creek Limestone	Gray, coarse-grained, crinoidal limestone. Extremely thin and mainly covered in the FVMM.	6-8
	Keyser Formation	Gray, fine- to medium-grained limestone; coarse-grained crinoidal limestone; thin brown sandstone; fossiliferous. Extremely thin and mainly covered in the FVMM.	75±
Silurian (409-439 million years ago)	Tonoloway Formation	Dark-gray, laminated, argillaceous limestone with thin, yellow-weathering shale partings; fossiliferous. Extremely thin and mainly covered in the FVMM. Excellent exposures in excavation to 19th century spring across VA-678 from Elizabeth Furnace.	50-100
	Wills Creek Formation	Greenish-gray, calcareous silty shale; brown weathering, gray, calcareous, sandy siltstone; gray fossiliferous limestone thin maroon shale; fossiliferous. Extremely thin and mainly covered in the FVMM.	60-150
	Bloomsburg Formation	Maroon, ferruginous sandstone, siltstone, shale, and mudstone; gray sandstone; carbonaceous shale; fossiliferous.	100-400
	McKenzie Formation	Yellowish-brown shale. Extremely thin and mainly covered in the FVMM.	0-75
	Massanutten Sandstone	Cross-bedded medium grained white quartz sandstone, locally conglomeratic (quartz pebbles). Thin black organic shale containing plant impressions of some of earliest of terrestrial pants. Fracture surfaces commonly rusty brown (Figure 10, p. 29)	700-1200
Ordovician (439-510 ma)	*Taconic orogeny. Deepening of Appalachian basin that slowly filled with turbidites moving southward. Deformation focused in New England but with some effects in Central Appalachians. Some erosion before deposition of Silurian formations above from the FVMM. Major extinction of many life forms at the end of Ordovician.*		
	Juniata Formation	White, chocolate, and red sandstone. Eroded away after Taconic orogeny in the Massanutten Mountains area. Present on Great North Mountain and westward.	Combined thickness:
	Oswego Formation	Greenish-gray brown weathering fine-grained sandstone; tan shale; conglomerate. Eroded away after Taconic orogeny in the Massanutten Mountains area. Present in North Mountain and westward.	450-500
	Martinsburg Formation	Black shale and limestone; interbedded greenish shale and lithic sandstone (turbidite) (Figure 24, p. 50, Figure 83, p. 138). Fossiliferous. Graptolites (Figure 60, p. 103), brachiopods common near top on the Massanutten Mountains. Older formations are beneath the Martinsburg within the FVMM area.	3200±

Chapter 9. Geologic History

The events of eternities ago may seem as having little bearing on the present day Southern Appalachians. Yet you miss much about them, much that is momentous, if you are unaware of their antecedents, from which their unbroken descent spans 250 million years.

–Charlton Ogburn, 1975[82]

Introduction

From geologic time to stratigraphy, we have set the stage for the final story: the region's long and varied geologic history, a subject already briefly touched upon. Historical geology reconstructs the character and sequence of physical and biological events that took place during the long development of Earth. It draws upon the evidence from rocks, minerals, fossils, and large-scale features. Modern methods also involve detailed laboratory studies, such as the chemical composition of rocks, radiometric dating, and paleomagnetism. It is an integrative science bringing together information from many disciplines. Historical geology is anchored by uniformitarianism, the idea that the present is the key to past.[83]

South of the Equator

By comparing the geological structure of both sides of the Atlantic, we can provide a very clear-cut test of our theory that this ocean region is an enormously widened rift whose edges were once directly connected or so nearly as makes no difference.

– Alfred Wegener, 1928

The way in which we view Earth history has changed drastically over the past 40 years, but began long before then. Alfred Wegener (1880-1930), the multifaceted German scientist noted for his work in meteorology,

---

[82] Carlton Ogburn, *The Southern Appalachians – a Wilderness Quest* (New York: Morrow and Co., 1975), p. 72.
[83] This is not, however, as simple as it may seem. The laws of physics and chemistry are viewed as having always been valid, but many ancient settings and specific processes may not be observed today.

glaciology, and astronomy, proposed in 1912 in a detailed exposition that the continents had slowly drifted together into a gigantic landmass about 300 million years ago. He termed this megacontinent Pangaea ("all land"). His famous book, entitled "*The Origin of Continents and oceans*," dealt, however, with far more then drifting continents. To this day, it remains a model of a thorough and creative analysis. His views contributed to a major change in ideas about the Appalachians, ideas that would be corrected and improved upon.

Wegener would write four increasingly improved books on continental drift, the last in 1928, two years before his death on the Greenland icecap.[84] Each book added new supporting evidence to counter the widespread criticisms of his ideas. Twenty-nine years later, Wegener's ideas were barely mentioned in the introductory geology courses required during my first year at Johns Hopkins University in 1957. We read from Yale geologist Carl Dunbar's 1948 then widely used textbook on historical geology.

Dunbar appreciated the need for some sort of connection between the continents because of the similarity of fossils from the continents of the southern hemisphere. Even though well aware of the theory of continental drift, he wrote in 1948 "Land bridges between the southern continents appear to have existed from early Paleozoic time till the middle of the Mesozoic, and then began to break down." Wegener's name does not appear in Dunbar's book—an otherwise stimulating and exciting entry book into the marvels of Earth's history. Dunbar's land bridges would become continents in contact, and his break down a result of the rifting apart of Pangaea in Wegener's scheme of things.

Beginning in the late sixties, such views of a static position of continents and oceans throughout time were banished. Studies of the deep-sea floor revealed that the ocean basins are, geologically speaking, very young and constantly changing shape. Also, rocks retain the orientation of the earth's magnetic field when they form. Magnetite-rich lava flows are particularly useful for this purpose because they retain a strong signal of the field in which they crystallize. Rocks formed at the Equator register that the magnetic field was oriented parallel to Earth's surface, those at the poles, straight down. Thus, sensitive laboratory instruments can determine the latitude at which a rock forms. Radiometric dating of the same sample

---

[84] The last edition is available now in paperback: Alfred Wegener, *The origin of continents and ocean basins* (New York, Dover Publications, 1996), translated from the German by John Biram from the 1929 final version.

allows determination of the time at which the Earth's magnetic field had been at that latitude.

This information, combined with fossil and geologic evidence, allows reconstruction of the likely location of continents and oceans through time. So, as we walk along ridges capped by the Massanutten Sandstone, think of a world geography in which the central Appalachian region was about 30° south of the Equator, and rotated 30° clockwise. Think, too, of a barren landscape, covered here and there by small plants that would later give rise to the amazing diversity of plants. Fish and invertebrates flourished in the seas, yet few animals inhabited the land, except for the first scorpions, flightless insects, and whatever made the tracks and burrows in the Massanutten Sandstone. The lack of vertebrate fossils in non-marine rocks indicates that they had yet to adapt to living on land. The world was strange in still another way. There were about 421 days in a year as indicated by growth rings in Silurian corals and brachiopods.[85]

Wilson Cycles and the Breakup of Pangaea

The continents and their margins are the pieces of a puzzle that shift location and change shape through geologic time. There are a number of patterns to this process. For example, the Atlantic Ocean[86] had formed and then closed at least twice. The cycles of creation of a giant continent followed by its breakup is termed a Wilson Cycle, first noted in a paper in 1966 by J. Tuzo Wilson, a Canadian geophysicist (1908-1993). The geological evidence for these two repetitions is clear on both sides of the North Atlantic.

Let's examine first the evidence that an ancient continent rifted apart to form the first Atlantic Ocean, the proto-Atlantic. The Precambrian and Cambrian rocks of the Blue Ridge and eastern Valley and Ridge include a great sequence of 800 million year old basaltic lavas and volcanic sediments that comprise the Catoctin formation, so beautifully exposed in Shenandoah National Park in Virginia. A hike to Stony Man Mountain in the central section provides an impressive view of some of the lava flows. These flows have compositions indicative of hot spots and their underlying thermal plumes, such as that beneath Yellowstone National Park today.

---

[85] S.J. Mazzullo, *Length of the year, Silurian and Devonian Periods* (Boulder, Colorado: Geological Society of America Bulletin, 1971) v. 82, p. 1085-1086

[86] But can we call the ocean before the Atlantic the Atlantic? Names like proto-Atlantic and the Iapetus Sea have been used for the ocean that separated Laurentia (an earlier and slightly different-shaped North America) from its once-joined fragments in the late Precambrian.

The formation of gigantic domes over hot spots is probably a good mechanism for the first stage of initial break up of a large continent. The lithosphere shatters along great rift faults that radiate from the domes, connecting and then joining the hot spots together.[87] The lithosphere, impelled by gravity, then slides away from the rift faults, rift valleys form and widen, eventually deepen, and an ocean basin is produced. Wilson also proposed this idea. It is an idea that I find reasonable and attractive. In the light of hotspots and continental breakup, we can imagine the Catoctin hotspot as one of a number that led to the inception of the first Atlantic.

The story does not end here. Deposition of sand and mud in the lower Cambrian deeply buried the Catoctin lavas as the region slowly sank. In places, cobbles and even boulders were violently washed by streams and rivers onto the rift floors. Conglomerate layers (conglomerates are rocks with abundant pebbles and even cobbles) at the bottom of the first of the Cambrian formations, the ridge-forming Weverton Formation, named after Weverton, Maryland, are evidence of this earliest event in what would be the 250 million year rock record left in the vast Appalachian basin.[88] The earliest of these deposits are non-marine, reflecting deposits typical of rift valleys. By the Middle Cambrian, sands and then carbonate grains, some containing marine fossils, record the transition of the region into a continental shelf—the proto-Atlantic became a full-fledged ocean.

Wilson noted the twofold creation and destruction of oceanic lithosphere and continental assembly involving the Appalachians. He noted that the continents bordering the North Atlantic came together twice to form supercontinents. The last assembly happened first during the Permian Period to form Pangaea, and a much earlier one during the late Precambrian to form what was much later termed Rodinia. The most recent supercontinent, Wegener's Pangaea, produced dramatic effects both on the biological and physical systems of the Permian Earth. The greatest extinction of life occurred during the Permian. Was it related to the many changes in climate and geography caused by the formation of Pangaea?

Disrupted fragments of continental lithosphere fit together best along passive margins, where their shape has been preserved since continental

---

[87] The lithosphere is the outermost rocky layer of Earth. It is brittle and carried along on the mobile denser, and plastic asthenosphere. The lithosphere is thin and dense under the oceans (oceanic lithosphere; about 70 km thick) and thicker and less dense under the continents (continental lithosphere, ca. 70-200 km or so thick).

[88] The Appalachian basin has much the same meaning as the Appalachian geosyncline. A geosyncline is a large down warping of the lithosphere in which thousands of feet of sediments have accumulated. Volcanic deposits, as well, occur in some geosynclines, but not abundantly in the Appalachian basin.

fragmentation. Passive margins are within plates, most now far from active spreading zones. They are termed passive because they are simply carried along passively as the plate moves: neither earthquakes nor volcanoes scar them. The Atlantic margins of North and South America are classic examples of passive margins. On the other hand, active continental margins, such as western margins of North and South America, are constantly changing in shape because of faulting, magmatism, and, at times, additions of other continental plates, all tending to obscure their original outlines.

The continents are now far from a new convergence. The major landmasses and major oceans are about opposite one another (antipodal) on the globe, and oceans cover about 71% of the surface. Earth's major oceans extend northward from Antarctica as if they were gigantic gulfs between the continents, defining the three great oceans of Earth, the Atlantic, Indian and Pacific. Another peculiar feature marks the distribution of land and oceans: 67% of the land area is in the northern Hemisphere. The gigantic landmass of Eurasia, although smaller than Permian Pangaea, has been greatly enlarged by the merging of India with Eurasia. It will enlarge still more when, in all probability, the Mediterranean closes, and Africa becomes sutured to Europe. Eurasia is now as large as the Paleozoic mega-continent of Gondwanaland. However, North and South America, Antarctica, and Australia are far from converging.

Rodinia

A little over a billion years ago, convergence of continents created the recently postulated megacontinent of Rodinia. The evidence is in the Precambrian rocks of the world, such as those that are tens of thousands of feet beneath the Fort Valley and, remarkably, exposed at the surface in the Blue Ridge due to uplift and thrust faulting (Figure 80, p. 135 and Figure 81, p. 136). Rodinia is the focus of many recent studies, and most geologists working on its reconstruction in time and space are far from agreement. Geologists Kah and Bentley edited a major book on Rodinia, and wrote: "The astute reader will note that there is no consensus on what Rodinia looked like, precisely how it assembled, or even when these events occurred."[89]

The problem is a difficult one because the farther back we go in time, the more fragmentary the geologic record. Nonetheless, the evidence is clear

---

[89] L.C. Kah and J.K. Bartley, *Rodinia and the Mesoproterozoic earth-ocean system* (Precambrian Research, 2001), v. 111, p. 2.

that Rodinia was broken apart in our area in the late Precambrian. As happens when the lithosphere is broken apart, volcanism, rift valleys, and earthquakes occur. We were near an active plate margin involving continental rifting and eventually seafloor spreading. The active margin was to the east (modern directions). Shifting and rotating plates constantly change our location relative to the geographic co-ordinates, appearing in speeded-up time as the shore does from a turning boat.

For most of the late Precambrian and Paleozoic, what would be the Fort Valley was south of the Equator and, in the Precambrian, rotated up to $180°$ clockwise! (Figure 82, p. 137, and Figure 84, p.140). One of the most bizarre proposed locations was near the South Pole during part of the Ordovician period, leaving a record of continental glaciation. That event happened before deposition of the rocks of the Fort Valley or Massanutten Mountains. Possibly the most widespread glaciation in geologic history was about 600-700 million years ago and is evident in the ancient glacial deposits of the Mount Rogers area of the Southern Virginia Blue Ridge, and in rocks of similar ages all over the world. Indeed, some have speculated that glaciers reached even the Equator, and have called this the time of the "Snowball Earth".[90]

Rifted Continents and Seafloor Spreading

Continental margins developed on the broken edges of the fragments of Rodinia as they were slowly carried away from the newly developing seafloor-spreading centers. The new ocean has been termed the Iapetus Sea, and is analogous to our modern Atlantic. Its margin, in particular, was similar to the modern margin of the Atlantic: a passive margin as it was no longer a site of earthquakes, volcanism, or folding. It was passively carried apart from a central seafloor-spreading center.[91]

The mid-Atlantic Ridge that neatly splits the Atlantic Ocean is like that of the ancient Iapetus Sea. The modern ridge is a chain of submarine volcanoes, rift valleys and mountains that continues to widen at a rate of up to an inch a year. The ridge reaches above sea level at Iceland, where the volcanism, earthquakes, and rift faulting provide a readily visible display.

[90] A detailed account, including evidence of many shifts from ice house to greenhouse conditions in this time interval (600-700 million years ago) are described on the web by Paul F. Hoffman and Daniel P. Schrag at http: //www-eps.harvard.edu/people/faculty/hoffman/snowball_paper.html
[91] For an introduction to the subject see W.J. Kious and R.I. Tilling, 2003, *This dynamic earth: the story of plate tectonics*, available at http://pubs.usgs.gov/publications/text/dynamic.html

Exploring the dynamic mid-Atlantic Ridge was a major part of my research between 1964 and 1974. I spent one month on the *Research Vessel Atlantis II* (now a tender for the deep-sea submersible Alvin), and one month on the *R.V. Thomas Washington* dredging and mapping. By the mid-seventies, attempts to drill deeply into the mid-Atlantic Ridge began. In this attempt, I spent four months at sea with a team of other scientists on the Drilling Vessel *Glomar Challenger*.

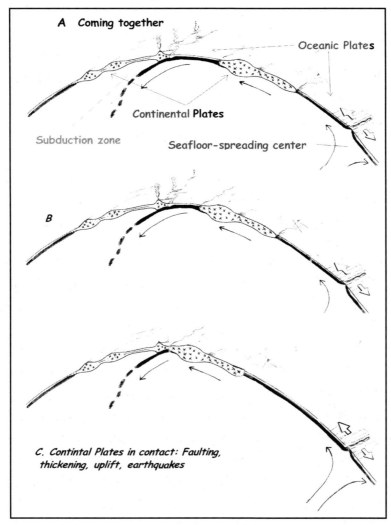

Figure 78. Simplified collision between two continental plates along a subduction zone, as happened to generate the Appalachian Permian Alleghenian orogeny.

We had a long shot at drilling into the mantle, which is at much shallower depth beneath the oceanic crust than under continental crust (7 versus over 30 km). Broken drill strings and stuck drill bits stopped us from getting anywhere near the mantle. But our success was great. Long nights and days on the drill-rig floor yielded unforgettably exciting discoveries. We learned a great deal about the lava flows and intrusions that make up the mid-Atlantic Ridge and how seafloor spreading works.

The oceanic lithosphere is normally reabsorbed into the mantle and therefore vast expanses of it are gone. Thus, it is by examining the modern seafloor and the processes by which it forms that we learn how ancient ocean basins took shape and the nature of their relationships to the continental lithosphere. Continental lithosphere, because of its thickness and low density, is not absorbed into the mantle and thus "floats" on the denser asthenosphere. Although fragmented, deformed, intruded, covered by magma (molten rock), and reassembled, the continents contain Earth's oldest rocks. Now, let's leave Rodinia and seafloor spreading, and examine one of the major consequences of the breakup of Rodinia.

The Great Carbonate Bank

Limestone ledges in fields and road cuts, buildings of limestone blocks, caves, and limestone quarries are all hallmarks of the Shenandoah Valley surrounding our study area. Such phenomena are witnesses to one of the greatest limestone deposits on Earth. As briefly mentioned before, this deposit is a major global sink (or trap) for carbon dioxide in the minerals calcite and dolomite. Carbon dioxide is an infrared-absorbing greenhouse gas that would otherwise accumulate in the atmosphere, consuming any life-giving potential, as has happened in the very hot, carbon dioxide-rich atmosphere of Venus. It behooves us, then, to honor and give thanks to Earth's immense carbon dioxide traps of limestone and dolostone deposits.

How did this vast deposit come about? It began when a tremendous thickness first of sandstone and then of limy mud were deposited on the edge of our broken continent of Rodinia as it trailed away from the Iapetus seafloor spreading center from the middle Cambrian to the middle Ordovician periods. These deposits became the Great Carbonate Bank that underlies not only much of the Shenandoah Valley of Virginia but its northward extension across the Potomac, where it is known as Maryland's Great Valley, and on into Pennsylvania, forming the Cumberland Valley.

However, we come now to the change that is directly reflected in our local rocks. Continental fragments that had rifted apart began to converge once again in the Ordovician period. With that convergence, the great interior Appalachian basin took shape and with it, the deposition of the Martinsburg Formation, and the end of deposition of the Great Carbonate Bank. These changes heralded fundamental modifications of the ancient Appalachian setting.

Shifting Basins: Changing the Flow Directions of Rivers

Modern rivers in our study area make their way to the east, albeit by tortuous paths. Flowing east, their waters eventually reach the Chesapeake Bay and finally there merge with the great Atlantic. But it has not always been so. During the time of deposition of the Massanutten-Fort Valley rocks, the rivers flowed the other way: from east to west, depositing their waters and sediment into the vast interior Appalachian basin. Although mainly inland, evidence indicates connections to the world oceans when the basin was below sea level.

At times, the interior basin was a shallow sea, at times a vast flood plain, crossed by meandering rivers. Slowly the basin sank, partly from the weight of the sediments slowly filling it, sometimes deepened by rising sea level. The sea thus retreated and advanced over the basin with each shift in the global sea level, changes in the rate of sediment deposition, tectonic uplift or subsidence. When the deposition rate exceeded the rate of subsidence, the sea margin retreated to the west, sometimes in front of growing river deltas (Figure 79, p. 133). These deltas grew into the Appalachian basin at various times during the Paleozoic, each evidenced by a clastic wedge, an westward-thinning deposit of mud, silt, sand, and, near the eastern source, gravels (Figure 9, p. 27). The oldest of these wedges is in the southern Appalachians, and grew during the Middle Ordovician. Three more would grow as deltas spread westward from the rivers of Appalachia.

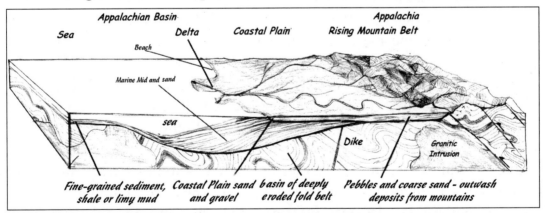

Figure 79. Generalized components of the Appalachian basin at a time of a growing delta with highlands on Appalachia undergoing erosion.

Speculations on Subsidence and Uplift

The rocks of the Appalachian basin and of Appalachia show unmistakable evidence of changes in sea level relative to the land. This can happen solely from subsidence and uplift of Appalachia and of the Appalachian basin, or from global changes in sea level (eustasy). Such global changes can result from the melting (causing a sea-level rise) or growth (causing a drop in sea level) of continental and polar glaciers. Sea level too depends on the volume of the ocean basins. The volume can decrease during time of high seafloor spreading rates. This is because new oceanic lithosphere is hot and expanded (lower density) than old lithosphere. Thus, at the time of a increase in seafloor spreading rates, the volume of the ocean basins decreases, causing a rise in sea level.

In the Piedmont province, we find in many places the high-pressure mineral kyanite, an aluminum silicate used in the ceramic industry and often forming beautiful blue bladed crystals, in metamorphosed sedimentary rocks. Such high pressures are generated by burial beneath tens of kilometers of rock. So, we have evidence of burial and thus of subsidence. Their exposure at the surface, where we may see and sample them, means thousands of feet of rocks have been eroded away. For this to be so, burial must have been followed by uplift. Although perhaps not as great, subsidence and uplift also mark the geologic history of our study area.

These ups and downs of Earth's surface are related to changes in the thickness and density of the crust. The thicker and lower the density of the crust[92], the higher the elevations. The crust beneath the Himalayas, for example, is both thick and of low density, thus the great elevations of the mountains and high plateaus. The crust beneath the ocean basins is thin and made of denser rocks, and so is at much lower elevation, far below sea level.

Let's explore the mechanism that results in changes in elevation. The elevation of the Earth's surface has to do with buoyant forces. Buoyant forces are those exerted on a body immersed in a fluid of a different density. If negative, the body will sink, if positive it will rise. Ice cubes float in water because they have a lower density than liquid water, and thus have positive buoyancy. Isostasy is the theory which views Earth's surface elevations in this way. In simplest terms, the elevation of Earth's surface at a given place is a function of the density and thickness of the underlying crust. Stated in another way, isostasy interprets the crust and possible parts of the upper mantle as a series of "floating" blocks, sometimes moving independently of one another, on a denser and ductile mantle. The height to at which they float depends on their density and thickness. The mantle is not

---

[92] The crust is the upper part of the lithosphere, the lower part is the upper mantle. Density changes in the uppermost mantle can cause changes in elevation at the surface.

a fluid yet can behave as a slowly moving ductile solid material when under stress. A ductile solid is one that can deform and flow without breaking. The asthenosphere on which plates move is viewed as a ductile (plastic) solid.

What processes can cause the crust to change its density or thickness? Small plates converged with the larger North American plate (termed Laurentia) in the Ordovician. Convergence leads to plate thickening and rises by three processes:

(1) Forceful via thrust faulting and plastic flow at depth,

(2) Volcanism and magmatic intrusion, adding new mass to the crust, and

(3) Heating of the crust, which causes expansion and thus a decrease in density.

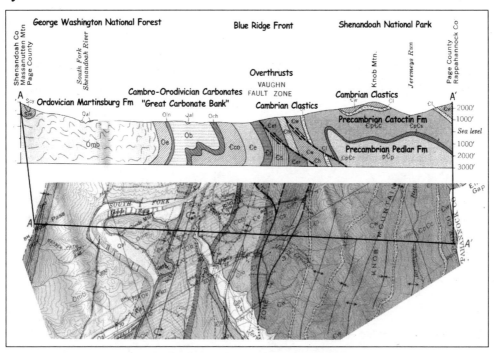

Figure 80. Overthrust of the basement of the Appalachian basin south of Front Royal.[93]

The crust and the uppermost mantle form the upper brittle layer of Earth—the lithosphere, or outer shell that is the plates of plate tectonics. Subsidence of the crust can be caused by a thickened adjacent mass. In this case, sinking hypothetically was caused by elastic bending of the eastern margin of the Appalachian basin adjacent to thickened Appalachia crust. The

---

[93] Modified from geologic map by Rhesa M. Allen, Jr., *Geology and Mineral Resources of Page County* (Charlottesville, Va., Virginia Division of Mineral Resources, Bulletin 81)

greatest thickness of sedimentary rocks is along the eastern margin of the basin, supporting this idea.

This mechanism has been proposed to explain the subsidence of the eastern Appalachian basin during deposition of the Ordovician Martinsburg Formation. Here's that explanation: Appalachia's lithosphere thickened from plate convergence and over thrusting. The added mass caused the adjacent eastern part of Appalachian basin to bend, reaching far below sea level. Figure 80 (p.135) and Figure 81 show over thrusting that occurred much later during the Permian orogeny that directly thickened the lithosphere of the Appalachian basin itself.

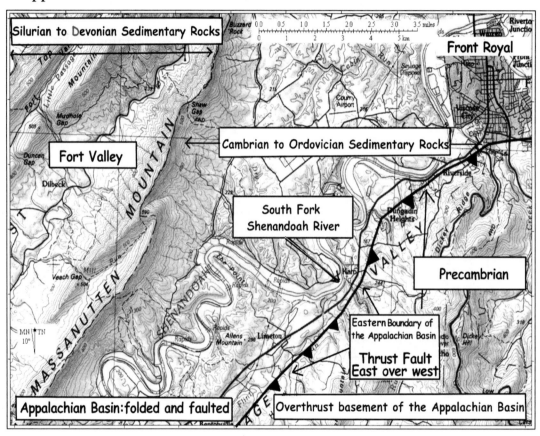

Figure 81. Inferred cross section of Blue Ridge Front showing probable large Permian overthrust fault of the Blue Ridge rocks over the younger Paleozoic rocks of the Appalachian basin in Shenandoah Valley near Front Royal, all now deeply eroded.

How can we account for the fact that the Appalachian basin, including the Valley and Ridge and Allegheny Plateau provinces, are, on the average, mountainous? The great highs along the Blue Ridge and the Great Smokey Mountains also need an explanation. Uplift, initially a maximum over the now low-elevation Piedmont province, seems to have slowly migrated westward. Is it that the crust, thickened during the Alleghenian orogeny, is slowly rising in response to temperature rise, causing expansion, hence a lowering of density, hence a rise? Heat flows very slowly in the crust (rock is a good insulator), and there may be a post-deformation lag in the temperature rise (from radiometric heating?) of crust thickened by thrust faulting and folding. This explanation is easy to imagine for the highly deformed Blue Ridge and Valley and Ridge provinces, but not for the seemingly less deformed Allegheny Plateau.

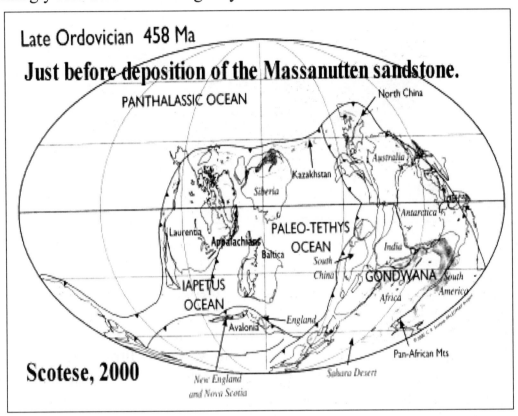

Figure 82. Position of the continents in the Late Ordovician, approximately the time of Martinsburg Formation deposition. Note that Laurentia (the core of North America) was south of the Equator. Modified from ©Scotese, 2003.[94]

The Taconic Disturbance and the First Uplift of Appalachia[95]

Paleozoic mountains rose in Appalachia during the Ordovician to the northeast of our area, and folding and faulting occurred in the northeastern

---

[94]Christopher R. Scotese, *Atlas of the earth history* (Arlington, Texas, Paleomap Project, 2000). There are a number of flip charts and other graphics indicating plate locations through time at www.scotese.com
[95]The term disturbance is often used for orogeny. Disturbance, although rarely used today, is a more graphic and explicit term because the slow accumulation of sediments in the Appalachian basin was disrupted, or disturbed, along with and connected to Appalachia, the land to the modern east

part of the Appalachian basin as well. The existence of these Ordovician mountains is evidenced in eroded folds exposed to the north in eastern New York. The folds were eroded and then buried beneath Silurian sediments, including coarse gravels. These sediments correlate with our Massanutten Sandstone. The mountains of that time no longer exist. They were completely eroded by the middle Silurian and covered by a sea that moved over the flat, eroded surface.

Figure 83. Folded shale from the Martinsburg Formation collected from road cut at the intersection of VA-340 and VA-55 just north of Front Royal.

The Ordovician mountain building episode was named the Taconic disturbance (or orogeny) after the Taconic Mountain Range of eastern New York, where the rocks give a clear record of its former existence. Its effects are found from Newfoundland, through the Maritime Provinces of Canada and New England, and as far south as New Jersey. The folds and faults, though, of the Taconic disturbance did not reach as far south as the Massanutten Mountains. There was uplift, though, and some late Ordovician sediment found to the west is absent here because of erosion during and after this uplift. This erosional unconformity dating from the Taconic disturbance is between the Ordovician Martinsburg Formation and Massanutten Sandstone and is best seen along the Fort Valley Road where it enters the Valley, and along the Buzzard Rock Trail at its overlook of the Fish Hatchery (Figure 12, p. 31).

At these places, a hard sandstone layer of the Massanutten Sandstone abruptly overlies soft shale and sandstone with brachiopod fossils of the upper Martinsburg Formation. Remember, too, that here you have the contact between rocks of two momentous geologic periods: the Ordovician and Silurian.

The topographic sharp step upward from the Martinsburg Formation to the Massanutten Sandstone at the north end of Massanutten Mountain on the Buzzard Rock Trail (Figure 12, p. 31) is indeed a monumental step in geologic time. Over that interval, in the upper Ordovician, there was one of the greatest extinctions of life on Earth. Such extinctions on a global scale are termed mass extinctions. Over 100 families of marine organisms and over one-half of all the brachiopods and bryozoans of North America disappeared. It is speculated that this is because many of the continents drifted very near or even over the South Pole. The marine fossils (brachiopods) in the shale fossils at the top of the Martinsburg at this same step in the Buzzard Rock Trail reminds me of the early controversies as to how mountain tops had once been seafloor, a subject recently explored by geologist Alan Cutler.[96]

Massanutten Sandstone Story

Let's focus now on the story of the Massanutten Sandstone, without which there would be no Massanutten Mountains. Sand and pebbles were washed west and southward from the Taconic (Ordovician) highlands at the beginning of the Silurian period and would lithify to the Massanutten Sandstone, including some conglomeratic beds. The Shawungunk, Medina, Tuscarora, and Clinch sandstones are of similar age and origin. All refer to a vast deposit that records the erosional degradation of the Taconic mountain range to the northeast. The Shawungunk formation, nearest the range, and now underlying part of the Appalachian Trail in Pennsylvania, is made of gravel (cobbles) and sand (Figure 52, p. 93) and, overall, coarser than deposits to the west.

At the sandstone's western extremity, far distant from its source, deposition was in a shallow sea as evidenced by marine fossils. Most of the eastern deposits (near land) are, however, non-marine. They are rich in the tracks and burrows of yet unidentified freshwater life forms. These trace fossils can be found just about anywhere in the float or outcrops of the Massanutten formation.[97] Various types of these markings were discussed and figured in Chapter 6.

---

[96] Alan Cutler, *The seashell on the mountaintop: a story of science, sainthood, and the humble genius who discovered a new history of the earth* (New York, Dutton, 2003)
[97] Float refers to rock fragments that have worked their way to the surface during down-slope movement or soil turnover of a mixture of large and fine rock fragments produced by rock weathering. Where there are no outcrops, it is the sole indicator of the rock that underlies the slope or surface.

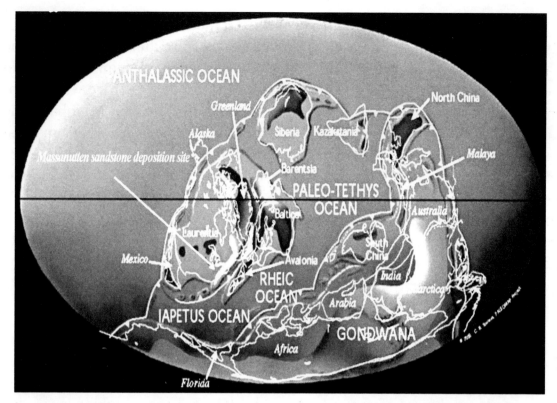

Figure 84. The Middle Silurian world, near the time of deposition of the Massanutten Sandstone, about 425 million years ago. Modified from ©Scotese, 2003.[98]

Black, shaly beds are scattered amidst the light-colored sandy and pebbly beds. A careful look at these reveals impressions of minute plants, looking like small plant stems. ***These are among the oldest known terrestrial plant fossils.*** Before these, fossil evidence reveals that plants were simple marine forms. Once adapted to land, these plants diversified into a great number of new species that, in turn, led to the vast coal swamps that would develop about 100 million years later, and to the land plants of the modern world. What life forms, if any, covered the surface before the first emergence of land plants?

The Greening of the World

There cannot be a more important event than the greening of the world, for it prepared the way for everything that happened on the land thereafter in the evolutionary theatre.

–Richard Fortey, 1997[99]

---

[98]Christopher R. Scotese, *Atlas of the earth history* (Arlington, Texas, Paleomap Project, 2000)

Since the discovery of these Silurian fossils, still older evidence of land plants has been uncovered, placing the emergence of plant life onto the land in the Ordovician. Simple marine plants, marine alga, were their ancestors. The onset of terrestrial plants is now detected by searching for fossil spores with characteristics indicating wind transport, and therefore an origin on land.

Figure 85. Models of a Silurian eurypterid, an early arthropod scout of the land, and of some of first land plants. Diorama in the Smithsonian's National Museum of Natural History, Hall of Ancient Life.

The first plants had to adapt to living beneath a bright sun, and thus death by drying out was a constant threat. Plants survived partly by evolving a waxy coating that reduced water loss. But such a coating reduced the flow of gases in of carbon dioxide in sunlight and oxygen at night, and out of oxygen in sunlight, and carbon dioxide at night, a necessity of photosynthesis. To regulate drying, the plant evolved stomata, minute pores that regulated the movement of gases in and out of the plant by a ring of cells that could contract or expand, triggered by the plant's needs. This armor allowed plants to safely spread, multiply, and diversify on land. Yet, survival on land required other innovations. Large marine plants are buoyed up by water, while those on land are in air—effectively, "heavier", requiring a stiff, more rigid stalk if they are to grow upright. A robust root system also is needed to provide water and nutrients from the soil. In the sea, these can be obtained directly from seawater.

---

[99]R. Fortey, *Life: a natural history of the first four billion years of life on earth* (New York: Vintage Books, 1997), p. 137.

Plants then, as now, are food for animals, and so there was a burst of new animal life on land. Indeed, the abundance of such a diversity of animal traces on the beds of the Massanutten Sandstone is evidence of the first stages of this evolutionary explosion of life on land. An immense reserve of space had been opened up, and new species began to claim each habitable land niche.

Figure 86. Plant fossil fragment in Massanutten Sandstone road cut on the Fort Valley Road (VA678), Passage Creek Gorge.

The Sea Returns and the Acadian orogeny

There rolls the deep where grew the tree,
O Earth what changes hast thou seen!
There where the long street roars hath been
The stillness of the central sea.

–Tennyson

Marine fossils reappear in the Bloomsburg Formation[100] in the Fort Valley amidst deposits of the clastic rocks on top of the Massanutten Sandstone. It grades upward into limy mud, later to be limestone. The sequence of shallow water deposits ends with the deposition of the Ridgely Formation. In

---

[100] Excellent exposures of the Bloomsburg Formation are near the southern end of the Sidewinder Trail near Elizabeth Furnace on the south side of the first small valley crossing.

the Fort Valley, the Ridgely forms ledges of a pitted sandstone and in places conglomerate that are commonly exposed on top of the limestone sequence and before the Needmore Formation. In the Little Fort Valley, these thin beds of quartz-pebble conglomerate (Figure 50, p. 90) are common in float around Powell's Fort Camp. The pits are probably from solution of calcite materials; some of the casts look as it they may be from dissolved brachiopods. There is a disconformity, a break in the record, between the Ridgely and the overlying Needmore Formation.

The Acadian orogeny then influenced deposition of the Needmore (shale), Marcellus (black shale), Tioga Bentonite (volcanic ash and shale), and the Mahantango (calcareous shale) formations, all containing marine fossils. The Devonian period in the Fort Valley is mainly represented by the comparatively thick shale, mudstone, and siltstone of the Needmore and Mahantango Formations. Marine fossils, especially brachiopod shells, are common in these. Both have calcareous layers, and, along with the Marcellus Formation, may contain hard, calcite-cemented roundish concretions that, as mentioned earlier, are often mistaken for dinosaur eggs![101] Layers rich in fossils in the Mahantango Formation are readily found in a road cut at the intersection of VA-771 and VA-678, about 8.5 miles south of Waterlick (Figure 19, p. 41), and elsewhere throughout the Fort Valley.

Figure 87 shows that there was a subduction (convergent) zone south of the margin of Laurentia (later to be a core of North America). Regardless of the details of where these volcanoes were, great eruptions produced thick layers of volcanic ash that fell into the Appalachian basin to the northwest and are preserved in the Devonian Marcellus and Tioga Bentonite (*Figure 87*, p. 144).[102] The Acadian orogeny dramatically affected New England and eastern Canada, and, less strongly, our area.[103]

Folding, Faulting, and Earthquakes: The Assembly of Pangaea

The Valley and Ridge Province is folded and in places faulted. Most of these structures were created during the Late Permian Alleghenian orogeny, the third major orogeny that affected our study area (previous were the Taconic and Acadian orogenies). This event, more than any other, uplifted, folded,

[101] See footnote 24, p. 37.
[102] Modified from ©C. Scotese (2000).
[103] This Acadian orogeny is detailed technically in D.C. Roy and J.W. Skehan, *The Acadian orogeny: Recent studies in New England, maritime Canada, and the autochthonous foreland* (Boulder, CO., Geological Society of America, 1993), Special Paper 275.

and faulted the Appalachian basin, ending over 300 million years of sedimentation. The flow of rivers took their modern west to east direction.

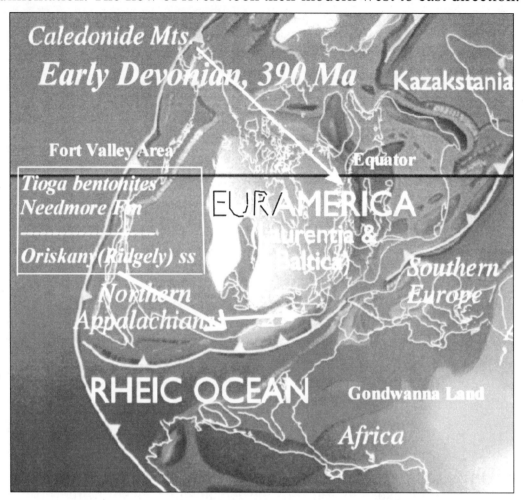

Figure 87. Fort Valley area in the Early Devonian, after deposition of the Massanutten Sandstone and before the deepening and mud influx of Needmore to Mahantango Formations.[104] *The line with upward pointing triangles marks the location of a zone of volcanoes (a volcanic arc) along a subduction zone just south of ancestral North America, and the source of the volcanic ash in the Marcellus and Tioga Bentonite.*

The Coastal Plain and Continental Shelf received the debris from the erosion of the rising Permian mountains. At that time, the region was near a zone of continent-continent convergence. Earthquakes were common along such a plate boundary, as they are today in the Himalayas.

---

[104] See footnote 98, p. 140.

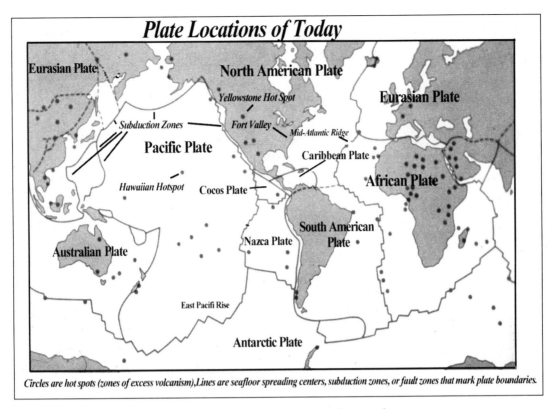

Figure 88. Major plates of the modern world, and some hotspots.

Let's stop our Appalachian story for a moment and examine some principles of plate tectonics. What exactly are "plates"? In the sixties, the theory of plate tectonics was developed from evidence from many fields of science. Detailed surveys of the ocean basins, however, more than anything else, clinched the theory. The ocean basins were found to be very young, geologically speaking, mainly less than 200 million years (remember Earth is about 4,600 million years old, or 4.6 billion years old). Seafloor spreading creates the oceanic lithosphere. The oceanic lithosphere is dense and thin (@30 km thick) compared to the continental lithosphere (up 100 km thick). The lithosphere is broken into many fragments, the plates of plate tectonics, by motions in the more plastic, hotter, underlying zone, termed the asthenosphere (described also on p. 133). Plate tectonics simply refers to these ideas and many more connected with the mechanisms and consequences of interactions between the mobile asthenosphere and the overlying brittle plates of the lithosphere.

Figure 88 (p. 145) shows the plates of today. Earthquakes and volcanism cluster at plate boundaries. We are safely located near the middle of the North American plate. This was not always so. The great Permian Alleghenian deformation marked the time when a plate margin—the zone of convergence of North American and the bulge of Africa—brought frequent and some undoubtedly large earthquakes, like we see in the Himalayas today, a zone that marks the convergence of the continental lithosphere portions of the Indian and Asian plates. As the ocean basins grow along zones of seafloor spreading, roughly equal areas of seafloor descend back into the mantle along the subduction zones, typically delineated at the surface by deep-sea trenches, and so the Earth does not expand. The continental portions of plates, again, although thickened, as in the Himalayas, do erode, much of their rock being deposited into interior or marginal basins. The basin rocks then may be folded and faulted upward again by new orogenies (plate convergence, or collisions[105]), but remaining in the plates because of their low density.

The Folds

The great Massanutten synclinorium diagrammed in Figure 93 (p. 150) helps to follow what is described below. A small anticline underlies Green Mountain in the northern part of the Fort Valley and is bordered on the west in turn by a small syncline (the Little Fort Valley syncline) that contains softer rocks, that by differential erosion led to the formation of the Little Fort Valley. The projecting "finger" ridge that underlies Signal Knob is the last vestige of the Massanutten Sandstone along the axis of the Little Fort Mountain syncline to the north.

Short Mountain (Figure 89, p. 147) is a small syncline to the west of and isolated from the other Massanutten ridges. The ridge is just southeast of Woodstock, with its northern end just south of the Edinburg Gap. Erosion has removed all but this small strip of the resistant Massanutten Sandstone. Short Mountain's cross-section brings to mind the vast amount of material that has been eroded from the Appalachians over the past 245 million years or so. The total amount is probably over 10,000 feet here. This erosion began in earnest when the slow convergence of Africa, Europe, and North America produced the great folds, faults, and uplift of the Alleghenian Orogeny.

Signal Knob marks the northwestern end of the outcrops of the Massanutten Sandstone (Figure 91, p. 148). Green and Three-Top Mountains merge at Signal Knob where they wrap around the south-dipping axis of the Little Fort Valley syncline.

---

[105] The term "collision" implies a rapid event in terms of our day-to-day experience, whereas plate convergences are slow, centimeters per year. Thus, the word collision, gives, I think, the wrong impression yet is commonly used for plate convergence.

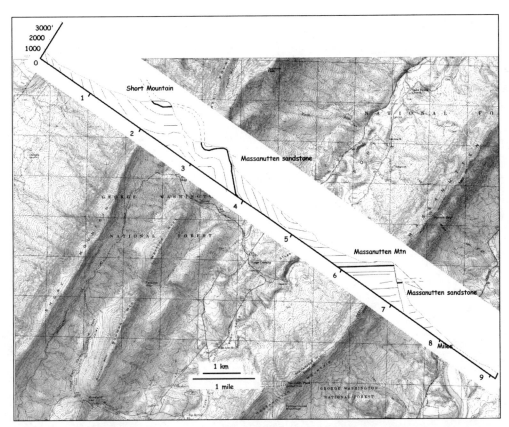

Figure 89. Inferred cross section that explains Short Mountain as a deeply eroded syncline, with just a bit of the resistant Massanutten Sandstone ridge-former left along the ridge crest.

Figure 90. South end of Short Mountain from VA-11 near Mount Jackson. Cliffs of The Knob are of the Silurian Massanutten Sandstone in flat-lying beds at the base of the Short Mountain syncline.

147

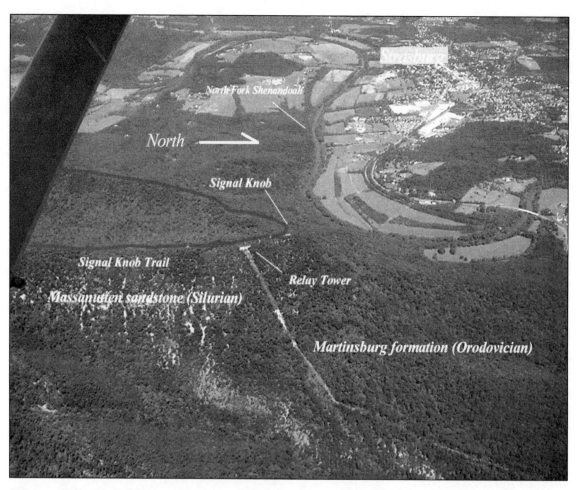

Figure 91. Aerial view of the northwestern end of the Massanutten Mountains, including Signal Knob. Signal Knob is the end of the Massanutten Sandstone in the Little Fort Valley syncline.

There is an anticline within the northern part of the area between Green Mountain and Massanutten Mountain. The anticline plunges south and the exposures of the Massanutten Sandstone disappear beneath younger rocks south of the Bear Wallow Trail. From the eastern part of the Bear Wallow Trail, you can see to the north the Massanutten Sandstone etched out, and appears like the back of a great whale rising from the sea.

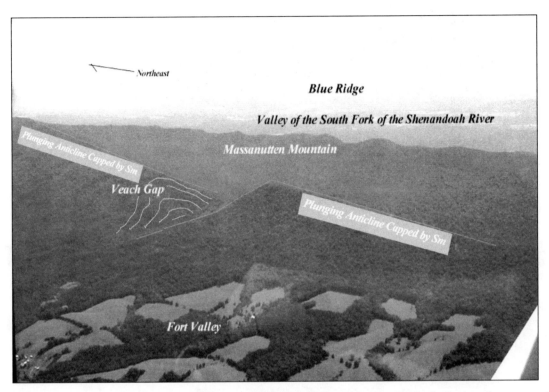

Figure 92. Aerial view of Veach Gap. Veach Gap is eroded through a small anticline that plunges southward and is underlain by the Massanutten Sandstone (Sm).

The peculiar double mountain of Veach Gap (Figure 92, p. 149) and Massanutten Mountain reflect a "wrinkle" in the eastern Massanutten synclinorium (Figure 93, p. 150). The Veach Gap Trail cuts through a southward plunging anticline and then crosses a small syncline that is marked on the east by Massanutten Mountain. Interestingly, the small Veach Gap syncline is symmetrically opposite the Little Fort Valley syncline as shown in the cross-section.

The cross-sections of Figure 8 (p. 26), Figure 89 (p. 147), and Figure 93 (p. 150) are, of course, oversimplified. Figure 8 (p. 26), in particular, shows that the motion that caused the folding was compression of the layers from the east to west. There are also immense faults associated with this compression, mainly caused by gravity sliding—the down-slope slippage of the sedimentary layers off a rising region to the east.

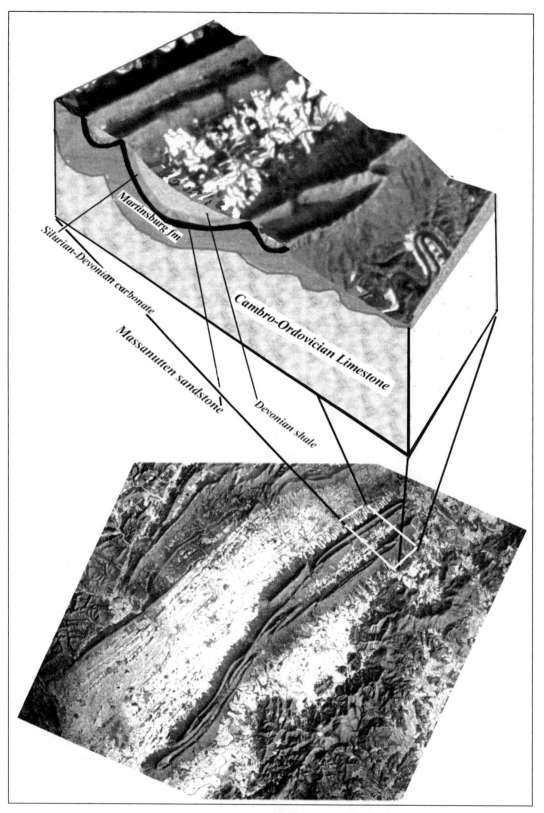

Figure 93. Cross-section through the Fort Valley and northern Massanutten Mountains revealing the folded interior—the great Massanutten synclinorium. Section includes Veach Gap on the east and the Little Fort Valley on the west.

150

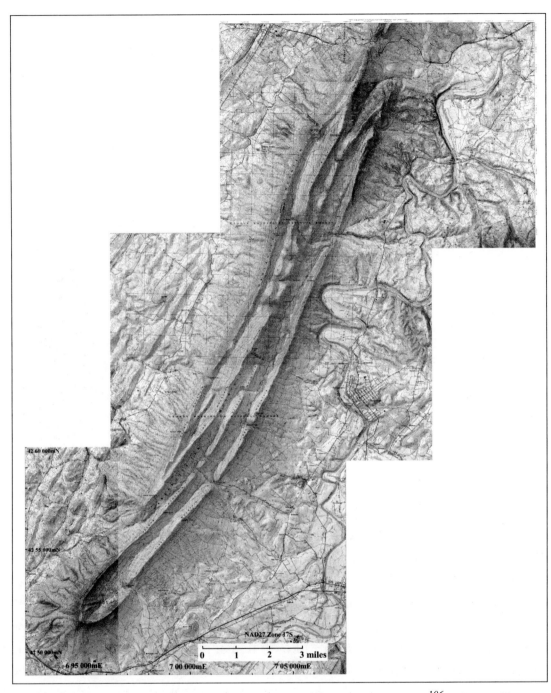

Figure 94. Southern portion of the Massanutten Mountains.[106] *The valleys are smaller and the ridges higher than in the northern half, reflecting tighter folding.*

[106] Modified from TOPO! [©,] Mid-Atlantic USA (2000), Disc 3. Shenandoah. ©National Geographic Society. Seamless digitized maps compiled from the U.S. Geological Survey 1:24000 topographic maps. Other topographic figures used herein were similarly composed using the TOPO[©] digital maps.

Figure 95. The Grand Canyon, Arizona. View is from the Havasu Indian Reservation on the south rim. The Grand Canyon, Arizona, sedimentary rocks have remarkably escaped the kind of intense folding that characterizes the Appalachian orogen.

Figure 95 shows the beautiful stratigraphic sequence in probably the most spectacular rock exposure on Earth—the Grand Canyon of the Colorado. Here, the sequence of Paleozoic and Mesozoic rocks have escaped the intense folding and faulting like that affecting the Valley and Ridge Province of the Appalachians. This type of regional uplift is termed epeirogeny. The rocks are Precambrian to Mesozoic in age. Most of the sedimentary rocks are shallow marine and subaerial sediment.

Faults

No major faults are exposed at the surface in the area. However, one or more large, nearly horizontal thrust faults probably underlie the area, such as the eastward extension of the North Mountain fault. This great fault is exposed at the surface along the west side of the Shenandoah Valley west of

Woodstock and extends northward through West Virginia and south to central western Virginia. It dates from the Allegheny orogeny and is typical of many great gravity slides that are far more common in the southern than in the central or northern Appalachians. The North Mountain thrust fault developed from the westward sliding of an immense slice of the eastern Appalachian basin, probably off the rising Blue Ridge, during the final assembly of Pangaea.

Figure 96. Anticline in Devonian shale on Fort Valley Road (Va678) 0.5 miles south of King's Crossing.

Figure 97 shows deep scratches and grooves (termed slickensides) that form on fault surface as one side grinds against the other. They are common in most outcrops, but especially in hard sandstone and quartzite. Steps in the slickensides reveal the relative motion of the fault blocks. The scratches in Figure 97 show a nearly horizontal motion and that the side in the image moved to the left relative to the one that has broken away (note the right-facing steps on the right side of the outcrop).

Figure 97. Slickensides (scratches) on a fault surface in quartzite of the Massanutten Formation along the Signal Knob Trail.

Historic Earthquakes

Our study area is relatively safe from major earthquakes because it is in the center of the North American plate, far from the active volcanic-earthquake margins of the mid-Atlantic Ridge to the east, and the Cascade-San Andreas boundaries to the west (see Figure 88, p. 145). Nonetheless, large earthquakes have rumbled through the area, the largest being those of 1811—1812 generated over a thousand miles to the southwest near New Madrid, Missouri (Figure 98, p. 155).

This episode of earthquakes involved at least 1,874 felt quakes around New Madrid between December 16, 1811 and March 15, 1812.[107] The most

[107] James L. Penick, *The New Madrid earthquakes*, revised edition (Columbia, Missouri: University of Missouri Press, 1981).

intense were during the weeks ending December 22, 1811, and January 26, February 2, and February 9 of 1812. In central Virginia (Figure 98, p. 155), these reached between magnitude V and VI (5 and 6) on the modified Mercalli scale, a qualitative scale based on felt and observable motions. Magnitude 5 corresponds to quakes felt by nearly everyone, many are awakened, and some dishes and windows are broken. Plaster walls may crack and poorly balanced objects fall. Church bells may ring, trees, poles and other tall objects may be tilted, and pendulum clocks may stop.

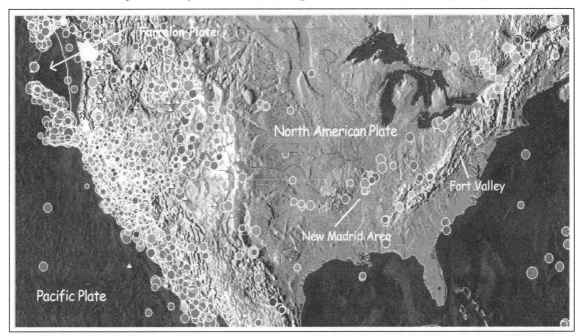

Figure 98. Over the past 40 years (1963-2003) no earthquakes with a magnitude greater than 4 (Richter scale) have occurred in or near the Fort Valley.[108] Most U.S. quakes are along the western boundary of the North American plate. The New Madrid area, Missouri, continues to be the site of many weak earthquakes and was the source of the great 1811-1812 earthquakes strongly felt in the Fort Valley.

Such motions were insignificant compared to those at New Madrid, where even well built wooden and masonry structures were destroyed. The maximum magnitude of quakes at New Madrid was estimated as 10 on the Mercalli scale. Three shocks reached this magnitude during the weeks ending December 22, 1811, and February 9, 1812. These were

---

[108] Program that generated this map is by Alan F. Jones and is available on the web at http://www.geol.binghamton.edu/faculty/jones. Alan Jones has provided a marvelous service in this program that is so useful for learning or teaching about earthquakes. His accompanying program showing seismic-wave propagation is equally useful for learning about Earth's interior.

unquestionably felt in the Fort Valley, although I have not found any historical record of their passage.

The New Madrid earthquakes are not along a plate margin, and so it is not immediately obvious how they fit into the simplified ideas of plate tectonics and earthquakes so far mentioned. They belong to a class of earthquakes that are quite common within plates (intraplate earthquakes, note them on Figure 98, p. 155). I have recorded a number of these in central Virginia on the Geology Study Center's seismograph. The New Madrid area may be on an active rift zone, but one of limited extent.

Earthquake intensity decreased far less with distance in the great New Madrid quakes tha n it does for California quakes. This is explained by noting that the Eastern and Midwestern U.S. crust is solid, hard, and lacks the fractures of the intensely faulted and shattered rocks of plate margins that more effectively absorb the energy of earthquake waves.

Summary of Geologic History

Events and settings during the Ordovician, Silurian, Devonian, and Permian Periods have, in particular, left a record in the region. Although there are no Permian rocks here, the folding and faulted record deformation of the late Permian Period—the Alleghenian Orogeny. Since the Permian, the region has been eroded, with episodic uplift. There are four major settings recorded in the Fort Valley and nearby areas (others are recorded elsewhere in the Appalachians):

1. Rodinia and the Iapetus Sea (Precambrian to mid-Ordovician).

- Formation of a continental margin by rifting of Rodinia.
- Eruption of lavas and other volcanic rocks associated with a sub-continental hotspot (late Precambrian Catoctin formation of the Blue Ridge Province, a process probably connected with the breakup of Rodinia).
- Rivers flowed from west to east (modern directions) into a newly forming Iapetus Sea.
- The Cambrian to Ordovician Great Carbonate Bank of the Shenandoah Valley formed on the continental shelf on the broken edge of Rodinia as the Iapetus Sea grew.
- Beginning in the Cambrian, shelled marine invertebrates left an abundant fossil record.

2. The Appalachian Basin and Appalachia (Mid-Ordovician to Permian).

- Formation of the inland sea, the great Appalachian Basin, that existed from the Ordovician to Middle Permian Periods (most of the Paleozoic Era).

- Deposition in the Appalachian Basin left a wide variety of sediments, divided into fourteen formations recording:

  (a) An inland sea, open to the World Ocean, with turbidites (Late Ordovician Martinsburg Formation).

  (b) Erosion (Late Ordovician to Early Silurian) associated with the Taconic Orogeny.

  (c) Westward and south-westward advance of stream-deposited sand and gravel, creating a habitat for some of the first land plants (Early Silurian).

  (d) Advance of a shallow sea and deposition of limy mud, sand and conglomerate (Upper Silurian to Devonian), followed by a period of non-deposition and possibly erosion after deposition of the near-shore to beach sands and gravels of the Devonian Ridgely (Oriskany) Sandstone.

  (e) Volcanic ash (Middle Devonian) fell into a sea where mud was being deposited, producing fossil-rich to organic carbonaceous black shale and mudstone. (Needmore, Marcellus, Tioga Bentonite, and Mahantango Formations).

- Appalachia grew by the accretion of continental fragments that produced orogenies in the Appalachia borderland in the Ordovician (Taconic orogeny) and in the Devonian-Mississippian Periods (Acadian orogeny).

- During the Acadian orogeny, explosive volcanoes erupted along a volcanic arc south of the Appalachian basin, located south of the Equator (Figure 87, p. 144) and rotated about 30 degrees clockwise.

- A number of mountain belts rose sequentially as a result of these two orogenies to the east in Appalachia, followed by erosion of Appalachia to near sea level.

- River flow into the Appalachian basin after the Middle Ordovician changed from west to east, to east to west.

3. Forging of Pangaea, Central Pangaean Mountain Belt (Late Permian Period).

- Folding, faulting and uplift during the Permian Alleghenian Orogeny induced by the convergence of North America and Africa, destroying the great Appalachian Basin about 300 million years after its formation.

- Rise of a mountain range centered in the vast continent of Pangaea—the Central Pangaean Mountain range.

- All the folds and faults of the Fort Valley and Massanutten Mountains date from this time.

- Intense earthquakes were common.

4. Pangaea's End, Growth of the Modern Atlantic Ocean Basin, Erosion (Latest Permian to Present).

- Erosion sculpted the eastern mountains from the Late Permian (250 million years ago) to modern time.

- Volcanism and earthquakes occurred beginning about 40 miles east of the Fort Valley in the Culpeper Basin area during the initial breakup, with formation of rift mountains, fault-bounded basins, and basaltic volcanism, producing cones, flows, and intrusions.

- Rivers flowed in modern directions, reversing from east to west, to west to east.

- The modern Atlantic Ocean basin grew starting in the early Mesozoic, about 230 million years ago, and continues to widen today.

- Deep erosion formed mountains by differential erosion (etch mountains) in the Fort Valley and Massanutten Mountains with some periods of uplift.

- Over the past two million years, great continental glaciers have advanced episodically as far south as Pennsylvania and drastically affected the flora and fauna of our study area.

- The beautiful landforms of the area continue to form by differential erosion.

- For nearly 250 million years, the area has been above sea level, roamed first by Mesozoic reptiles, mainly dinosaurs, and then by mammals during the Cenozoic Era.

- Humans reached here from the Old World at least 12,000 years ago, leaving a clear record at the Thunderbird site just west of Massanutten Mountain.

Figure 99. Life in a Devonian sea like that in parts of the Appalachian basin at the time. Smithsonian's. National Museum of Natural History, Hall of Ancient Life.

Geologist Preston Cloud's remarkable book "*Oasis in Space*" contains an appropriate quote with which to end our story:

> Things are not what they seem. Terra is not all that firma. The everlasting hills wear down. What was once tropic has changed places with the once polar. Sea floor is on a perpetual return trip to its mantle source, rafting continents and microcontinents with it, to be reassembled in other places, times, and patterns.
>
> –Preston Cloud, 1988[109]

[109] Preston Cloud, *Oasis in space: Earth history from the beginning* (New York: W.W. Norton & Co., 1988), p. 193.

Figure 100. Gnarly roots of an old oak slowly rip apart an outcrop of Devonian marine limestone near Elizabeth Furnace.

Epilogue

Geology leads, inevitably, to a deep appreciation of our Earth, to the immensity of time, to amazing processes, and to the breath-taking beauty we find today in our natural landscapes and rocks. Could an artist's brush trace more elegantly the natural, delicate, form left as erosion has slowly etched the outline of the Massanutten Mountains? In the woods or in viewing the landscapes, it is easy to imagine the delight that all those naturalists of today and of the past have found here. It is easy to imagine too the many long-gone geologists who walk, ghost-like, with us over the landscape, gazing at rock outcrops, breaking off a piece with their hammer, looking at it with their hand lens, and wondering how it fits into the story they are writing in their mind. Every change of lighting brings out new, often puzzling features. The sparkling quartz crystals glimmer in sunlit rocks along the ridge-crest trails next to the puzzling markings of the Silurian trace fossils of the Massanutten Sandstone. And the imagination goes wild if one begins to realize what we now know about the travels of our continents, of locations far from our present one, and of the long march of landscapes, seascapes and their ever changing animal and plant passengers. Above all, though, we know that there are yet so many things to learn, things present for us to see, but their meaning not yet recognized. We remain endlessly fascinated and curious about what we find in the Massanutten Mountains.

Index

164

165

166

About the Author

 Bill Melson received geology degrees from Johns Hopkins University (BA) and Princeton University (PhD) and is a fellow of the Geological Society of America and the Mineralogical Society of America. With Brian Mason, he wrote the first textbook on *The Lunar Rocks* (Wiley and Sons) and served on NASA's Apollo 14 Preliminary Examination team. His writings include chapters in the Smithsonian's *Book of the American Land* (*Shenandoah Roots*) and in the Smithsonian-National Geographic book *Forces of Change* (*Global Synergies*). The ongoing eruptions of Arenal Volcano, Costa Rica, are a major subject of his current research.

Bill is a life member of the Potomac Appalachian Trail Club. He and his wife Judy McCarthy live on a farm built in 1835 enclosed by Massanutten Mountain on the east and Green Mountain on the west. Along with gardening and hiking, they have converted an old chicken house into the Fort Valley Geologic Study Center. He has two daughters, Mary Katherine and Amy Elizabeth, and two grandchildren, Amy's Sophie and Russell Gell.

Melson is geologist emeritus at the Smithsonian's Museum of Natural History, Washington, D.C., where he has led geology tours to the Appalachians for the Smithsonian Associates and other organizations for the past forty years. On the twenty-fifth anniversary of the Smithsonian Associates in 1990, Melson received the following commendation:

> A quarter of a century ago, Dr. William G. Melson began to lead tours for the newly created Resident Associate Program and to encourage other Smithsonian staff to make their experience and knowledge available to the fledgling organization. He has been a dedicated contributor to and supporter of the Program ever since. A born teacher who infects his students with a love of rocks, Dr. Melson seasons his science with a poet's vision, transforming stone and soil into a dramatic window on restless movements and awesome forces; and conveying the image of earth's geological matrix as a mother of us all. He is one of those rare educators who combines a warm and outgoing personality with a boundless enthusiasm for his subject and the skill to share his expertise with novice or dedicated geological student alike.